TRADITIONAL
Country Style

TRADITIONAL
Country Style

ELIZABETH WILHIDE

INSPIRATIONAL IDEAS
AND PRACTICAL TIPS FOR
EVERY ROOM

CONRAN OCTOPUS

First published in 1991 by
Conran Octopus Limited
37 Shelton Street
London WC2H 9HN

Reprinted 1993

EDITOR Denise Bates
DESIGN Peter Butler
PICTURE RESEARCH Kathy Lockley
PRODUCTION Julia Golding
EDITORIAL ASSISTANT Lynne Drew

British Library Cataloguing in Publication Data
Wilhide, Elizabeth
Traditional country style: inspirational ideas and practical tips
for every room.
I. Title
747

ISBN 1 85029 367 8

Typeset by Butler & Tanner Ltd
Printed and bound in Hong Kong

CONTENTS

THE COUNTRY LIVING ROOM SHOWS THE COMFORTABLE, INFORMAL SPIRIT OF COUNTRY STYLE AT ITS BEST. A ROOM SPECIFICALLY DEVOTED TO RELAXING IS A RELATIVELY RECENT DEVELOPMENT. IN PREVIOUS CENTURIES, THE ROOMS OF MODEST COUNTRY COTTAGES HAD TO SERVE MANY, MORE FUNCTIONAL PURPOSES.

INTRODUCTION

Where exactly is the country? Ever since we started to live in crowded towns and cities, the country has been a place to which we have been trying to return. In our minds, it is not so much a particular dot on the map, more of an idyll, a retreat from the harsh, necessary realities of daily life. For some of us the country might mean the Long Island shore, for others the Devonshire countryside, or the hillsides of Provence. But wherever we locate it, the country represents the same basic attitudes and approach to living.

One of the strongest appeals of country living is its informality. Country style is the opposite of grand, the opposite of any effect engineered purely to show off status or expense. Rooms are for living in, not for display; surfaces and finishes are robust, and nobody minds if they are a little worn and even shabby.

Then there is the comforting sense of continuity, of tradition. Real country life is not nostalgic, in the sense of recreating a fairy-tale past which never existed, but very much of the present, upholding practices which have stood the test of time. Country homes are full of vitality, alive with a thousand activities.

But by far the most powerful attraction is the sense of being closer to nature. Being in the country implies a contact with the natural world which is much harder to feel in the city. In the country nature is ever-present in all its seasonal changes: there is the opportunity to grow and enjoy a whole range of plants; while the traditional patterns and images of country decoration serve as a constant reminder of the outdoors.

Luckily, for those of us without thatched cottages, rustic farmhouses or country retreats of any description, these essential qualities and elements can be created anywhere. The true spirit of the country, with its appeal to the senses, its emphasis on natural things and materials, and its easy accommodation of the past, can be part of our lives wherever we are.

CHAPTER ONE

ROOMS TO WAKE UP IN

THE VERY ESSENCE OF A COUNTRY MORNING: AT THE MOMENT OF WAKING YOU OPEN YOUR EYES TO A VIEW OVER HILLS AND FIELDS; LIGHT STREAMS IN THROUGH THE WINDOW AND A FRESH BREEZE FLUTTERS THE CURTAINS. SNUG AND COMFORTABLE UNDER A QUILTED COUNTERPANE, YOU THINK ABOUT THE ATTRACTIVE PROSPECT OF A DAY SPENT OUTDOORS OR ENGAGED IN SOME AGE-OLD COUNTRY PURSUIT. THE ROOM IS BRIGHT AND CHEERFUL, THE FURNISHINGS PRETTY; EVERYTHING THAT YOU NEED FOR THE DAY AHEAD IS LAID OUT NEATLY.

A sumptuous country bedroom has butter-yellow panelled walls and a painted wooden floor decorated to resemble inlaid marble. The dramatic bed drapery is very simply achieved using plain striped fabric knotted and hooked to the wall.

For most of us, this is certainly a pleasant picture, even if it might seem an unattainable ideal, something to be savoured only during weekends in the country. But, like other aspects of country life, you need not necessarily be ensconced in a rural paradise to enjoy the same atmosphere. A room furnished with natural materials, filled with individual cherished possessions and suffused with natural light is achievable in any home.

urge most people have to holiday in countries where the skies are blue every day. To be gently awakened by the light rather than the shrill sound of the alarm or the drone of the clock-radio is a luxury most of us associate with holiday time. Natural light also makes an important contribution to the special qualities of a country bedroom.

If there is any flexibility in the way your home is arranged and you have the opportunity to choose which room to make your

How you begin the day will have a lasting effect on your mood and outlook. And one of the best ways of ensuring a good start is to create the ideal environment for this most important time of the day.

MAKING THE MOST OF NATURAL LIGHT
Light has a profound effect on our state of mind, an effect that can be partly gauged by the sudden lifting of spirits experienced when the sun comes out, or the irresistible

All-white decoration and furnishing is an unbeatable way of making the most of natural light (above). Touches of fresh greenery and the warm tiled floor prevent the room from being too cold-looking. A desk placed in the corner between the two tall windows benefits from light, air and views. Sunlight, filtered through louvred shutters, stripes the simple unadorned beds (right). The striped bed linen echoes the effect; a warm grey colour picks out the dado and architraves.

way in which the window is covered will determine the degree and quality of light admitted. Secondly, you can do a great deal to enhance the brightness of a room by a careful choice of colour for both decoration and furnishings.

A LIGHT TOUCH

In keeping with the country mood, the decorative scheme which you develop for your bedroom – the colours, patterns and textures – should enhance the effects of natural light and suggest an atmosphere of freshness and repose. Getting it right is a question of scale and tone. In the bedroom, more than in any other room, unfortunate consequences can result from only slight miscalculations: here colours which would merely seem bright in another context can look strident, patterns which would be interesting elsewhere can tire the eye. You do not want to be forced to remember the immortal and supposedly last words of Oscar Wilde: 'Either that wallpaper goes, or I do.'

In general, bedroom colours should not be too bright or overly intense. But if 'pastel' conjures up an image of insipid, washed-out or sugary shades, think again. Pale clear tones can be both luminous and subtle if handled correctly. Commercial paint manufacturers have widened their ranges considerably in recent years and there are now many excellent pale shades which are neither dreary nor sickly. Many of these fall into the category of tinted whites, or 'white with a hint of . . .' and all, even the cooler, bluer shades can be very effective in a bedroom. Although strong colours may look good at the end of the day, under artificial light, they

SPECIAL PAINT EFFECTS SUCH AS COLOUR WASHING ARE NOT A MODERN INVENTION. AS FAR BACK AS THE SEVENTEENTH CENTURY PROFESSIONAL DECORATORS WERE EMPLOYED TO USE WASHES AND GLAZES, AND MARBLING AND GRAINING TECHNIQUES.

bedroom, always pay careful attention to the aspect, or direction it faces. You may not want to wake up with the rising sun shining straight in your eyes, but a room which receives some direct light will always be warmer and more welcoming than one which doesn't. A north-facing room, especially if the windows are small or positioned high up the wall, will have a chilly, dark aspect that may well prove difficult to overcome.

If you don't have the choice – which is probably true in most cases – it is nevertheless important to make the most of the light which does exist. This can be accomplished in two ways. First of all, the can be oppressive first thing in the morning and for this reason it is usually better to stick to the lighter shades for the main surface areas and to reserve darker colours for accent and trimming.

If you are prepared to take a little extra time and trouble, a superb way of achieving a sense of depth and luminosity in the paint surface, without sacrificing brightness, is to adopt professional decorators' methods and to paint the walls in successive thin coats, each slightly different in tone. Layers built up in this way – thin coats of emulsion or 'washes', or thin coats of eggshell or 'glazes' – are translucent and subtle, and colour almost seems to float on the surface.

White, of course, is a natural choice for the bedroom. On the one hand, it goes well with the farmhouse look, with simple furnishings and forthright textures; on the other, it can also assume more of a classic appearance. White was an exceptionally fashionable colour for bedrooms in the Edwardian era; you can recreate this rather luxurious prettiness by setting off an essentially white scheme with a dainty rosebud paper or pale chintz. Lots of lacy pillows piled on a brass bedstead complete the look. If you can, try to avoid using standard commercial white paint, which has a blue tinge to give what manufacturers like to call 'brilliance'. Instead, aim to produce an aged, mellow white which goes so well with country walls and all their irregularities. Using plain trade white, which has no added tints, you can mix in small amounts of artist's pigments in earth shades to make an antiqued white which has none of that harsh brilliance. Old roughcast walls, aged but sound

Rose-coloured chintz with an upholstered bench and needlepoint rug in a similar, though not matching pattern, add up to a gentle, delicate bedroom scheme (far left). This dramatic attic bedroom with its skylight and tiny window needs only the simplest decoration – pure white – to draw attention to the architectural detail of the steeply sloping roof (above).

plaster, and even half-timbered ceilings all look good painted in this chalky warm colour – perhaps the nearest we can get to old-fashioned whitewash or distemper.

As far as patterns are concerned, a similar restraint should apply. What you want to achieve is an impression of liveliness, not a dense layering of motif on motif that can become suffocating. Country bedrooms often have a hint of the floral bower about them. The dainty charm of sprigged wall-paper, wonderful old chintz for curtains and loose covers, and twining leaf and flower prints all have a place here. You can add an element of strength and introduce some variety by combining floral patterns with a simple geometric, such as a stripe or small check. Pale candystripe paper works well with rosebud curtains; gingham combines effortlessly with large floral or leaf patterns.

A particularly strong element in country decoration is designs derived from folk art. These patterns have a fresh, naive quality which comes from the fact that they are often handmade, featuring traditional styl-ized motifs, such as hearts, flowers, stars and diamond shapes. Into this category come patchwork quilts, stencilled borders painted on the wall, colourful hook and rag rugs and cross-stitch samplers. Although these designs are often brighter than the muted shades typical of many floral patterns, provided every inch of the bedroom is not smothered with them, they can add a valuable and welcome note of cheerfulness.

An unusual curved and veneered bedstead, a mellow brick floor and old beamed ceiling are set off with jolting yellow distemper used on the rough plaster walls (right). Patchwork, needlepoint and kelim rugs make a glowing feature of the antique bedstead (far right, above). A deep open basket stands at the foot of the bed providing storage space for blankets and covers (far right, below). The sense of country harmony relies on muted colours, natural textures and a lack of ornament.

16

TURN REMNANTS, SCRAPS OF BRIGHT DRESS FABRIC, OR SNIPPETS FROM WELL-LOVED ITEMS SUCH AS A CHILD'S COT BLANKET INTO A PERSONAL TREASURE BY QUILTING. THE TRADITIONAL METHOD INVOLVES BINDING THREE LAYERS — TOP, INTERLINING AND BACKING — TOGETHER WITH A PATTERN OF STITCHING. CONSULT PATTERN BOOKS FOR METHODS AND ENLIST THE HELP OF FRIENDS FOR A COMBINED EFFORT.

Tie-backs give curtains a neat, finished look. There are many styles: you can make your own from matching fabric, tie a wide ribbon in a bow, knot a scarf around the curtain, plait several widths of fabric together or use a gold cord or rope trimmed with a tassel. For a period look, sweep the curtain behind a metal hold-back.

Don't overlook the possibilities offered by textural variety when you are making up your mind about which colours and patterns to use. Texture is an important element in any room, but especially in the bedroom. When colours are pale, and patterns discreet, contrasts of texture can provide the extra dimension needed to prevent the decoration looking bland and uninteresting. Figured damask, broderie anglaise, woven rugs and throws, fringed shawls and fine embroidered pillowcases can all contribute to this enriching combination of textures. Textural variety is particularly pleasing on the floor. Carpeting, of course, is comfortable and warm under bare feet, but area rugs over painted or sealed and waxed floorboards are almost as comfortable and do not present such a uniform appearance. You might like

to copy the traditional Scandinavian idea of laying long woven runners around the perimeter of the bed or along main routes. Striped rag rugs are ideal for this purpose.

At the window

In any room, the window is a focal point and the way it is 'dressed' will inevitably attract attention. In a bedroom, window treatments often have other functions to fulfil. There may be the need for privacy, depending on what the window overlooks. You may want some protection from draughts; you may need to muffle the sound of the world outside. And there is nearly always the need to modify the light in some way, from filtering really bright sun, to total blackout for light sleepers. The best solutions provide some flexibility to suit different times of day and different require-ments. But as well as all these practical demands, what you hang at the window should look good. Venetian blinds are, for many purposes, supremely practical, but they are hardly an appropriate or attractive choice for a dormer window in a thatched cottage or for elegant sash windows in a Georgian farmhouse.

Country style, essentially, combines what are often considered to be 'natural' materials, motifs and themes with a traditional approach to decorating. In terms of window treatments, this usually means some form of curtaining rather than the bald simplicity of blinds on their own. Really grand, and specifically period effects are similarly out of place. In a country bedroom, look for a curtain style which, without being overly

Fine draped cotton softens the lines of this window, in a style suggestive of neo-classical window treatments (far left). The painted chair and table and unusual curved metal divan pursue the same period look. Even less elaborate, but equally effective are these simple lengths of semi-transparent fabric hung over a high brass pole (left). Chintz is a classic country fabric, particularly effective in window treatments when used unlined, allowing the light to come through (right). These sill-length curtains have been neatened with matching fabric tie-backs and a soft, gathered pelmet.

fussy, displays fabric in a soft, pretty way. Gathered headings, rather than crisp, con-temporary-looking pleats are more appro-priate. Delightfully informal and suitable for a wide range of fabrics, the gathered heading draws the material up gently to fall in soft, full folds. The curtain can be hung simply from a pole on wooden or brass rings; for a more feminine look, you might want to add a pelmet. Again, gathered fabric pelmets,

deeply recessed, as in an attic bedroom, you may want to fix the curtain pole or track to the outside of the recess; it is unlikely that there will be enough room otherwise to draw the curtain clear of the window so that it can operate properly. Whatever length the curtain is, to maximize light it is a good idea to extend the curtain pole or track beyond the window at either side so that the curtains can be pulled clear. In the same way, if you have a pelmet, make sure that you suspend it (and the curtain it covers) high enough above the window so that it does not obscure it but merely skims the top edge.

Less structured curtain styles – that is, those that do not require tracks, tapes, hooks or runners – also conjure up a country mood very well. Enchanting and pretty, they are generally exceptionally simple to make. The top edge of the curtain can be gathered in ruffles, or just loose tucks, and ties, bows or loops sewn on the back to suspend the curtain from the pole. The result invariably has a charming, rather rustic appearance.

Surprisingly, the lining of a curtain can also make a contribution to the way the room looks. Most people are familiar with the practical advantages of lining, but the decorative aspects of lining are just as important and have long been neglected. Although during this century, lining fabric has generally been restricted to off whites and creams, in earlier times, the lining could be brightly coloured or even patterned.

Coloured lining is a wonderfully subtle way of filtering light. Early sun shining through a curtain lined in yellow, for example, will suffuse a room with golden light. Pink lining will have a similarly

TRANSFORM THE LIGHT BY LINING CURTAINS IN A COLOUR. TRY YELLOW BEHIND A BRIGHT, FLORAL OR LEAF PRINT FOR A RICH BUTTERY LOOK; PINK FOR A WARM EFFECT. HOLD BOTH FABRICS UP TO STRONG SUNLIGHT TO ASSESS HOW THEY WILL LOOK TOGETHER. OR CHOOSE PATTERNED LINING FOR A PLAIN CURTAIN FABRIC – RATHER LIKE THE IMPACT OF A PRINT LINING IN A JACKET.

where the material is drawn up in the same fashion as the curtains, give a soft look. Avoid swags or severe pelmet styles, which are more at home in formal settings.

As well as the heading, the style of a curtain is determined by its length, which in turn will reflect the character of the room and the type of window. A cottage bedroom, with little casement windows, may look swamped if the windows are swathed in full-length curtains; sill-length would certainly be more effective here. On the other hand, a high-ceilinged Victorian bedroom, with large sash windows, demands full-length curtains simply to balance the proportions. Sill-length curtains in this context would look mean and skimped. If a window is

Lace is another good choice for a window treatment where privacy is not a major consideration (left). Panels of lace have been roughly tacked to this old casement window, set into crumbly whitewashed walls. It is often better to display lace flat, or gathered only slightly, so that the full detail of its pattern can be appreciated. This is also a delightful way to put an old lace shawl or table cover to use. A soft rose colour unites the different patterns in this peaceful country bedroom (below). Successful pattern mixing relies on some basic sympathy between each of the patterns; in this case, colour and type of motif. The effect is warm without being claustrophobic.

warming effect, while light blue will give a fresh, crisp tint. Naturally, the curtain fabric will also be affected, particularly if there is a great deal of white in the background of the pattern. Printed or patterned cotton lining was a common Victorian choice for a curtain whose main outer fabric was densely patterned or richly textured. You can make the most of the contrast by extending the lining over the leading edges of the curtains to make banding. Coloured or patterned linings can also transform the view from outside: think of the cheering effect of colour and pattern at the windows instead of the usual blank, neutral shades.

Curtains, however great their decorative potential, may not be enough when it comes to meeting all your practical requirements. In many cases, it may be necessary to combine curtains with fabric blinds or inner, lightweight curtains. Both fabric blinds and semi-transparent curtains can help provide privacy, as well as flexible light control without darkening the room to an unacceptable degree. The simplest solution and the most unobtrusive, is to combine curtains with plain fabric blinds such as roller blinds, or Roman blinds which pull up in neat folds. But equally effective and far more evocative is to hang light curtains in lace, muslin or any other semi-transparent material. Panels of antique lace with their filigree patterns or drifts of snowy muslin, cotton voile or fine net which billow out at the slightest breeze, are the perfect complement to soft gathered curtains. In the summer, you can remove the heavier outer curtains and leave the inner curtains in place. This strategy, apart from giving the room an instantly lighter, more summery feel, will also prolong the life of the main curtains and protect them from fading in strong sunlight. Otherwise, if draughts aren't a problem, and neither is privacy, you might wish to consider semi-transparent curtains as a year-round substitute for curtains made of a denser fabric.

Metal bedsteads with their painted roundels make a delicate filigree set against plain white walls. Something of the same effect is created by the stencilled border running at picture rail height. It is important to align stencilling with architectural features, as here, where the border meets the top of the door opening.

Bright light shining through these open-weave materials creates lively dappled patterns that seem to dance over the walls and ceiling – altogether a particularly attractive effect in a bedroom.

As far as the main curtain fabric is concerned, your choice should be made in the context of the colours and patterns you use elsewhere in the room. Bedrooms, traditionally, are 'upholstered' rooms, where there are likely to be fabrics in abundance.

BEAUTIFUL BEDS

Country beds are the most romantic of all. Given the choice, who wouldn't prefer to sleep in a four-poster, drawing the curtains against the night – or to start the day in an antique brass bedstead heaped with lace-trimmed pillows? Compared to the modern divan, traditional beds have character and it is this which makes them so appealing.

If the bed is to be the centrepiece of the room, it should be worthy of the attention. You may not be able to afford a real antique, but there are various ways of dressing up standard beds to give them a more distinctive appearance. Tester beds – the proper term for four-posters – were grand affairs. Heavy drapery, hung from a canopy or tester, curtained the bed, providing both warmth and privacy. At the same time, the quality and richness of the fabric and its trimmings eloquently testified to the wealth and status of the household.

Today bed drapery still gives a sense of security and enclosure, as well as carrying with it a hint of luxury. In a well-heated bedroom, there is no need for bed curtains to draw. Elegant columns of fabric hung from a plain wooden or metal framework or tied on with fabric bows can be made to fairly narrow widths and still be highly effective. Remember to line the 'curtains' since you will be viewing them from both sides. Other ways of suggesting the intimacy of a curtained bed are to drape fine muslin or net over an armature projecting from the wall over the bedhead, or to hang fabric like a mosquito net so that it encloses and frames the top of the bed.

A romantic country bed is the centrepiece of this high-ceilinged room (left). Snowy white bed hangings are combined with lacy pillowcases and a white counterpane. Bed drapery in white always looks fresh and delicate. Equally romantic and supremely feminine, a blue-grey bedstead is draped in filmy fabric suspended from the ceiling like a mosquito net (above). The colours used on the bedstead are extended to the other areas of woodwork in the room to provide unity.

Plain half-testers lined in blue gingham give twin beds a look of distinction (left). Dark wood mouldings emphasize the handsome proportions of the room. The robe hanging from a hook on the wall is reminiscent of the typical Shaker arrangement. A yellow wash over rough plastered walls and complementing floral chintz used around and on the bed, including the headboard, and at the window, give this room a fresh, spring-like look (below right).

A FEATURE OF TRADITIONAL SHAKER INTERIORS IS A WOODEN PEGBOARD RUNNING AT AN ACCESSIBLE HEIGHT ALL ROUND THE ROOM. MAKE A VIRTUE OUT OF NECESSITY AND USE A SIMILAR ROW OF PEGS OR HOOKS TO HANG UP NIGHT AND DAY CLOTHES, BAGS AND SCARVES, OR PRIZED POSSESSIONS.

Naturally, it all helps if your bed is distinctive in design. Reproductions of Victorian brass and painted iron bedsteads are widely available, as are the originals – metal bedsteads were made in great numbers at the end of the last century. There are also modern metal bedsteads which are equally handsome. In the same way, fine carved period wooden beds are collector's items but a variety of wooden bedsteads produced today are very sympathetic in style and can have individualizing touches added to them. For a homely country look you could paint or stain a plain wooden bed and subsequently distress the finish, or add decorations such as stencilled floral sprays or borders. Divans without headboards can be dressed up quite simply, too. Try hanging an embroidered cloth or a beautiful heirloom quilt on the wall behind the bed. A painted or carved panel salvaged from an old chest can also stand in as a headboard.

How the bed is dressed with sheets,

covers, quilts and pillowcases is all part of the picture. In the country bedroom, luxury is the luxury of simplicity and comfort. Frilly valances, satin coverlets and extravagant ribbons and bows are more at home in the boudoir. Opt instead for pure cotton or smooth linen sheets, freshly laundered and delicately scented with lavender, for plump continental quilts and eiderdowns encased in snowy white covers, for pillowcases edged in lace or broderie anglaise, or daintily embroidered with tiny daisies, forget-me-nots and intricate white-on-white work. Try traditional blue and white ticking to cover cushions and bolsters for a clean-lined look, or gingham in fresh shades of blue and green for a jaunty mood.

Express the mood of the seasons by changing bed covers and quilts. In the winter, pile the bed with knitted Afghan rugs and comforters, fringed plaid blankets or heavy woven throws. In the summer, substitute silky embroidered shawls, light cashmere blankets, quilted coverlets in the gentle colours of lavender and primrose, or mint green and pink.

The ultimate country bed cover must be a patchwork quilt, the product of hours of careful stitching, handed down and cherished over the years. Traditional quilts, often sewn by families or small communities of women, and commemorating such events as weddings or the birth of a child, are collector's items and increasingly expensive. If you have the time and skill you could make your own to one of the time-honoured designs, incorporating scraps of fabric, mottoes and motifs that have personal meaning. You might like to include a piece of your wedding dress, for example, or a snippet of your child's first nursery blanket. Simplified quilting, using the sewing machine, is not as fine as handwork, but very attractive results are possible nonetheless.

BEST FOOT FORWARD

Unless you have rooms to spare, the bedroom is likely to be the place where you dress and keep your clothes. But a room which is dominated by clothes' storage of one kind or another is not necessarily a very appealing place in which to spend time. You will need some strategy for screening the

bulk of your clothes, shoes, cosmetics and so on, while keeping what you use on a day-to-day basis readily to hand.

The country bedroom is the place for a whole range of traditional pieces of furniture, most of which are intended to function as clothes storage. Great mahogany wardrobes, antique clothes presses and huge carved armoires can provide capacious storage space for hanging clothes. Chests of drawers in all sizes can accommodate folded clothes, bedlinen, cosmetics, jewellery and other accessories.

Dressing tables, with curtained or drawer fronts, are the place to keep cosmetics, jew-

ellery and lingerie. Chests and ottomans at the foot of the bed can house blankets and covers. Laundry and other large wicker baskets are also appealing and suitable for this purpose. For accessories, such as shoes, hats and all those countless scarves and trinkets which accumulate over the years; a collection of hat and shoe boxes covered in pretty floral, striped or checked fabric or paper makes an attractive and practical display. Another good idea is a folding screen, covered in baize, paper or fabric; this can be a useful and attractive way of hiding a corner washstand, or of partitioning off a dressing area within the main bedroom.

Built-in storage is far from incompatible with country living and hiding clothes from view reduces the need for massive pieces of furniture which could cramp a small room. If you add a wall of cupboards, drawers and shelves, take care over the detailing to ensure that mouldings, catches and drawer pulls are in style. The cupboards can be painted to blend in with the walls – or even papered – or the wood attractively waxed or varnished.

The secret of decorating in the country style is to make use of all those items which are as attractive as they are useful, to create displays and collections around the home. In the bedroom, there are many different accessories to put on show – collections of gleaming silver-backed brushes, antique perfume bottles, beads, shawls, old hat boxes, leather cases and straw hats.

Old framed family photographs, a needlework sampler and a lovely mirror make a personal display alongside the bed (left). A handsome carved and painted wardrobe is a welcome addition to any room, providing ample space for storage without detracting in any way from the country aesthetic (above right). Wardrobes, although essentially intended for clothes storage, need not be confined to the bedroom. Fitted with shelves rather than a hanging rail they can be used to house a wide variety of other items. The Shakers, on the other hand, stored clothes and household goods by hanging them up out of the way on a pegged rail which ran around the perimeter of the room (below right). This arrangement is a good way of displaying and enjoying the appeal of simple everyday objects.

A NEEDLEWORK SAMPLER WAS A TRADITIONAL RECORD OF A GIRL'S LIFE AND SEWING SKILLS. YOU CAN DESIGN YOUR OWN, INCORPORATING A VIEW OF YOUR HOUSE, THE DATE AND YOUR NAME OR INITIALS. SAMPLERS ARE WORKED IN CROSS OR TENT STITCH ON EVENWEAVE FABRIC SUCH AS CANVAS OR LINEN.

Lyn Le Grice's Cornish Stencils

Tucked in a little valley close to Land's End are a farmhouse, an old mill and a group of outbuildings: Lyn Le Grice's Cornish home. Best known for her stencil designs, Lyn now has a wide-ranging practice as an interior designer, with international commissions which have included everything from decorating a stately home to designing a collection of textiles. Yet despite all the travelling her work entails, Lyn identifies strongly with this isolated part of Cornwall and draws great inspiration from the colours of the sea, the native plants and the granite landscape.

Her farmhouse bedroom is a tranquil refuge from the rich patterns and detail of her day-to-day work. The colours – muted greys and grey-greens – echo the changing colours of the sea; pattern is low key and unassuming. Behind the bed is an original piece of linenfold panelling, which was rescued by a friend from a builder's bonfire in London. The white folded linen which is draped above the bed in the form of a half-tester is something of a visual pun, but also suits very well the prevailing mood of simplicity. At the windows, deep set in thick walls as a protection from the strong winds of the peninsula, are curtains of the same plain white linen.

The floorboards show the faintest trace of colour: a thin wash of a shade somewhere between grey, blue and green was rubbed into the wood. A friend wove rag rugs in similarly muted colours of warm grey, beige and grey-brown. The walls, like many old country walls, were originally painted in limewash, tinted various shades. When Lyn cleaned them down, she revealed layers of blues and pinks

30

showing through in patches. She decided not to cover up the walls completely but to apply a thin coat of white distemper which merged the colours together. On top of the distemper she then stencilled a pattern of clumps of thrift, the maritime plant which is also known as the sea pink. The stencilling – pale pinkish flowers, bronze leaves and muddy grey-green hillocks – was very sparsely spaced across the walls. Since the work was completed, the basic chemical incompatibility of limewash and paint has caused peeling in places, but this slight degrading of the surface is in fact an effect which Lyn rather likes.

The stencilling in this room is a good demonstration of Lyn's belief that stencilling should be seen as an extension of the architectural qualities of a room, not merely overlaid as an afterthought. This concern with architectural qualities also informs other decorating decisions. In Lyn's living room, for example, which is shown on pages 168–9, she has used scaffolding planks set deep into the surface and washed with plaster to create a bookcase in sympathy with the rough walls of the room. Here in her bedroom, the nature of the stencil design is in harmony with its setting and suits the simplicity of the old distempered walls.

THE BREAKFAST TABLE

All too often in our busy stressful lives, breakfast is a perfunctory affair, a cup of instant coffee drunk standing at the kitchen counter, a piece of toast eaten on the run. There is no time for anything other than basic refuelling before the day begins in earnest. The problem is, of course, time — we often linger in bed until the last minute. But, paradoxically, getting up earlier can be more relaxing and refreshing in the long run.

If you allow extra time at the beginning of the day for an enjoyable breakfast, you will be giving yourself the best possible start.

Breakfast is a time for making a gentle transition from waking to full alertness, for clearing the mind ready for daily activities. For many people, it is a time for little rituals, a time set aside just for themselves. Others prefer to spend it in company, enjoying a lively exchange of family information before everyone goes their separate ways.

But whether you want to breakfast alone or in company, where you have breakfast will contribute to the atmosphere of the occasion. Different places in the home have their own advantages. For a family breakfast, there's nothing better than sitting round a pine table in the kitchen, informal and at the heart of things. For a quieter start to the day, you might want to set up a table in a sunny alcove looking out over the garden, or to take a tray to a window seat. For complete privacy, breakfast in your bedroom. Draw up a comfortable armchair by the window, or for the ultimate indulgence, breakfast in bed from a beautifully set tray.

Keep the table setting fresh and simple. Plain white linen, cheerful checked gingham or light floral patterns combine well with simple crockery in solid colours or rustic patterns, such as lively sponged designs. Look out for intriguing but amusing pieces to brighten up the morning – milk jugs shaped like cows, decorative egg cups, pretty leaf plates can all give a personal touch. And don't neglect that most important detail, flowers. First thing in the morning is not the time for heady scents or large bouquets overhanging the table, but a few fresh flowers give any meal a lift. Try a bunch of violets in an antique perfume bottle, or a few blooms from the cottage garden cut low so the heads float in a glass bowl.

The aromas of breakfast time are among the most evocative scents of all: fresh coffee, sizzling bacon, warm rolls baking in the oven. Breakfast appetites vary, but clean, fresh tastes help to wake you up, while subtle sophisticated flavours belong to later in the day. Most fruits are enjoyable at breakfast

Although the ingredients are simple, breakfast can be as appealing as more elaborate meals. This tempting array of homemade preserves, honey, fresh bread and fruit makes an ideal start to the day (left). Fresh juices flavoured with herbs are set out in a sunny corner, making a perfect breakfast drink (above). When the weather allows, it is particularly pleasant to breakfast outdoors.

and combine well with cereals for a healthy start. All kinds of breads and rolls, from nutty granary loaves and buttery croissants to crisp triangles of toast go well with little glass dishes of apricot or quince jam. For a more substantial meal, eggs in various forms are the traditional English standby. Add a sprinkling of chopped chives or fresh thyme, or slivers of smoked salmon to lightly scrambled eggs as a special touch.

THE FRESH TASTE OF FRUIT MAKES IT IDEAL EARLY MORNING FARE. THE TANG OF GRAPEFRUIT IS A CLASSIC BREAKFAST TASTE. MIX FAMILIAR AND EXOTIC JUICES FOR VARIETY, OR TRY FRUIT SALADS AND COMPOTES AS AN ALTERNATIVE TO WHOLE PIECES OF FRUIT. IN SUMMER, SPRINKLE CRUSHED ICE CUBES OVER CHILLED PIECES OF FRUIT FOR A REFRESHING ICED FRUIT SALAD.

CHAPTER TWO

THE WELL-TEMPERED HOUSEHOLD

IT IS A PARTICULAR FEATURE OF LATE TWENTIETH-CENTURY TASTE THAT WHAT WE MOST OFTEN FIND APPEALING ABOUT HISTORIC HOUSES IS JUST AS LIKELY TO BE 'BELOW STAIRS' AS THE GLITTERING PUBLIC ROOMS ON DISPLAY ABOVE. PERHAPS IT IS A LEGACY OF MODERN DESIGN — TOGETHER WITH A CERTAIN NOSTALGIA — THAT MAKES US APPRECIATE THE SIMPLICITY AND SERVICEABLENESS OF THESE WELL-RUN ROOMS, THE ENGINES OF THE GREAT HOUSES OF THE PAST. THEIR RELEVANCE FOR MODERN HOUSEHOLDS SHOULD NOT BE OVERLOOKED.

A large armoire with deep shelves trimmed in lace edging holds a quantity of crockery, tea services, tureens and dishes, glassware and table linen, everything neatly stowed, free from dust and easy to find when needed.

IN PREVIOUS CENTURIES HERBS WERE SCATTERED ACROSS BARE FLOORS TO COUNTERACT UNPLEASANT SMELLS AND GUARD AGAINST DISEASE. A MODERN ALTERNATIVE WHEN SPRING CLEANING IS TO PLACE SPRIGS OF FRESH HERBS SUCH AS ROSEMARY, THYME, MARJORAM OR BASIL UNDER RUGS AND CARPETS, OR IN DRAWERS.

NEATLY STACKED LARDERS, ROWS OF LABELLED bells indicating when assistance was required, stone-flagged mudrooms kitted out with racks for outdoor gear, cedar-lined linen rooms, with shelves of sheets folded and tied with ribbon – these all attest to the kind of peaceful and orderly existence of which dreams are made. Today's 'house-keepers' will not have a battalion of servants to help them; with luck, they may enjoy the co-operation of other family members. With so many demands on time, organization is the key to keeping the home running like clockwork. And to a large extent this means where you put things; in other words, storage.

GETTING ORGANIZED

The annual spring clean used to be a time when, as well as scrubbing the house from top to bottom, every nook and cranny was investigated, the contents of every cupboard turned out and inventoried and heaps of unwanted items discarded by the crateful. There is something to be said for this yearly marathon. The change of seasons imposes different demands on a household. Brighter days reveal dust in forgotten corners, dull, discoloured paintwork, and areas needing more urgent repair. Heavy winter curtains beg to be taken down and packed away. Cushion covers, bed covers and table linen can be changed for lighter, more summery versions. Winter wear can be retired for the next few months, while tennis racquets, croquet sets and barbecues can be dug out from their hiding places ready for summer activities. Even if you cannot afford to set enough time aside for a one-off spring-

cleaning session, or call on enough willing volunteers, it is still worth retaining this basic approach. It may take longer, but working through the various areas of the house in a methodical way will repay dividends in terms of space and ease of living.

Once a year is not too often to review your possessions and decide which ones are ripe for discarding completely, which can be retired for a while to an attic or store room, which now deserve to see the light of day or which can be put to a new use. Now is the time to get rid of all those clothes that have been outgrown, paperbacks and other books that you don't want to read again, the odd unhappy gift or bad buy. Anything which has been unused or even untouched for the past few years is probably just taking up house room and won't be missed. Jumble sales, church bazaars and charity shops can be the beneficiaries.

What goes back into deep storage – in the loft or attic, in a box room, garage, cellar or shed – should be clearly labelled or listed so you know exactly what you have and where it is. For the rest, you will need to find storage places which are well at hand but still out of the way. This can mean anything from converting forgotten corners, or adapting traditional pieces of furniture, to making a virtue out of a necessity and putting it all on display.

Entirely clad in pine panelling, this attic makes a dry, warm and attractive place to store old luggage and sports equipment. The contents of every loft are not always as antique, but a well-kept attic is an invaluable storage resource for things you don't want to throw away but don't need every day.

FORGOTTEN CORNERS

Space is tight in most homes, but, paradoxically, it is often the smallest that are the best organized. If you look around carefully, you are bound to notice places that could be put to work as storage areas. This may involve a degree of lateral thinking. For inspiration, think of shipshape cabins, where everything stows neatly out of sight, or old caravans, with their dual-purpose fittings – beds that turn into seats, or tables that fold down from the wall. Underused areas in most homes include the area under the stairs, on landings, under beds, and halls and entrance areas generally. Under the stairs is an ideal position for rows of shelves, built-in cupboards, or a cloakroom if the head height is great enough. Free-standing bookcases look good on landings, as do old chests filled with blankets or linen. You can store clothes which are out of season in trunks or cases under the bed to give more hanging space in your wardrobe. The space under a window seat could be converted into a cupboard; you could line a disused hearth with shelves. Corner cupboards and corner shelves can be tucked into odd places around the home. You can even construct dummy pilasters to provide hidden storage space in a drawing room.

The ultimate luxury is the storage room, which includes such evocative places as the linen cupboard – not today's humble airing cupboard but the grand walk-in affair of Victorian days, lined in cedar wood. Many older homes include tiny rooms which in former times would have been box rooms or pantries and which now can be put to good use as proper storage rooms. These

A DELIGHTFUL WAY TO ADD WITTY TOUCHES TO ANY ROOM IS WITH *TROMPE L'ŒIL* PAINTINGS. DRAW THE DESIGN ON GRAPH PAPER THEN CHALK OUT A GRID ON THE SURFACE TO BE DECORATED. THE DESIGN CAN THEN BE TRANSFERRED SQUARE BY SQUARE. AN ALTERNATIVE IS TO PROJECT A SLIDE ON TO THE WALL AND DRAW AROUND THE OUTLINES.

*Hallways make useful areas for storage. Here a
double row of wooden lockers painted to match the
woodwork could take a large amount of clutter,
relieving the pressure on space in the kitchen (left).
Free-standing or built-in cupboards can be tucked
into any odd corner. In this attic room, the fireplace
houses a wooden screen disguising a boiler and
cupboards are fitted into the alcove and under the
eaves (above). Witty paint effects such as* trompe
l'œil *chickens on the cupboard panels serve to
unify the arrangement.*

rooms, too small to be really habitable, can
nevertheless absorb a surprising amount of
clutter, dramatically freeing space in bedrooms, bathrooms and nurseries.

It is worth taking the trouble to make
these rooms attractive and practical so that
you enjoy using them. Put up proper shelves
and paint them; finish off cupboards neatly;
extend flooring and decorate the space

attractively. A storage room shouldn't be a place for abandoning junk, it should have a character of its own. If you are devoting the space to storing linen, make an attractive display. Tie up the sheets and towels in neat bundles with coloured ribbon and add sachets or bags of lavender. If there is enough space, you might also set up a small table and chair as a mending corner for carrying out on-the-spot repairs and darns. If the storage room is to be a cloakroom, or a walk-in coat cupboard, make sure that as well as hanging space there is a shelf for hats and gloves, a rack for boots and shoes, and a mirror.

ROSEWATER OR LAVENDER WATER PERFUME LINEN, TOWELS AND CLOTHES WITH A DELICATE SCENT. PUT A FEW DROPS INTO THE FINAL RINSE WHEN WASHING OR ADD A LITTLE TO THE WATER IN YOUR STEAM IRON.

Collections of similar objects or similar containers turn storage into display. Decoy ducks set up in a row on top of a line of small drawers give a lighthearted look to a kitchen storage area (far left, above). Hanging things from hooks keeps them out of the way but well on view. Metal baskets are ideal for storing onions, garlic and eggs – anything which benefits from the free circulation of air (above left). Neat rows of baskets, each in its proper place, are practical as well as appealing (left). Baskets are the most versatile country container; they can be used to store almost anything and look good on display. A collection of old painted and enamelled cooking pots and pans makes an informal group (above). A traditional form of storage is this painted wooden cupboard, pressed into service as a place for keeping table and other linen (right).

STORAGE WITH STYLE

It really doesn't matter what behind-the-scenes storage areas, such as lofts and cellars, look like, as long as they are efficiently organized, dry and clean. Storage on full view, however, needs to be in keeping with the style of your house. In the country interior, storage needs particular care. Many modern systems comprising shelving and prefabricated units would look glaringly out of place. Shelving supported on metal brackets that slot into aluminium uprights, mesh baskets on runners, and the ubiquitous matt black trolley are all modern storage standbys that simply don't make the transition to the traditional home at all happily.

Luckily, there is more than enough scope in other types of storage furniture to meet all possible needs. Many of the traditional pieces of furniture that we are familiar with today evolved to solve one storage problem or another. In many cases, they can simply be put to the same use today. A Victorian wardrobe will still provide capacious hanging space; a chest of drawers will take folded clothes or linen that can be stored flat. The oldest storage piece of all, the chest, dates back to the earliest days of furniture-making. Then, as now, it was a versatile item, housing everything from clothes and bedlinen to cups and plates. Few are fortunate enough to possess an antique carved chest, but a wide variety of similar pieces can provide the same flexibility. Pine blanket boxes are relatively common and fairly affordable; seaman's chests, steamer trunks, and wickerwork seats with upholstered hinged tops are all acceptable substitutes. Many of these can be painted to blend in

Old cupboards and fittings salvaged from a variety of different sources can be treated with a number of paint effects to help them blend into a domestic setting. This tall cupboard with ranks of drawers has been roughly painted and daubed with bold streaks to give it a lively look (left). Rough planked walls and bare floorboards make a supremely rustic background (above). In such a setting, an old wooden chest, with its slightly battered finish, and the painted, turned wooden shelves are the perfect storage pieces. Country style is tolerant of less-than-perfect finishes, signs of wear and tear and natural, unadorned surfaces.

with a colour scheme and even decorated with a stencilled motif to pick up on a decorative theme.

Instead of building in a cupboard, you might like to buy a free-standing one instead. Large country armoires can accommodate the entire contents of a linen cupboard, with the added bonus of looking attractive and perfectly in keeping. Plain wooden cupboards, occasionally with glass fronts, were typically used to store crockery, pots and cutlery. You can put them to the same use today, in the absence of a dresser, or fill them with a wide variety of other things, including books or toys. Bookcases come in a variety of sizes and styles, from large pedimented designs in fine woods to plain painted shelves intended for a bedroom. Built-in bookshelves lining alcoves or entire walls are very compatible with the country look; such shelving, of course, can be used for other things besides books, including records, tapes and games. Shelves can be painted to tone in with walls, or stained or varnished a dark wood colour. For a traditional finishing touch reminiscent of the country rectory, add scalloped or toothed leather edging along each shelf in crimson or green. Books and magazines also look good stacked on green iron or white painted metal garden staging.

Many antique tables or desks incorporate storage within their design. These include sewing or work tables, night tables (with a lower cupboard for housing a commode), 'secretaires' with upper bookcases, pigeon-holes and drawers, rolltop Wells Fargo commercial desks, and rent or drum tables, with alphabetically indexed drawers round the

Modern purpose-built shelving blends effortlessly with old fittings, providing ample storage in this kitchen (left). Baskets hanging from the ceiling are a traditional touch. Glass-fronted cupboards are a good way of displaying and storing glassware and china. Cups hanging on hooks make the most of the available space (above). The country dresser is a key storage piece, with just as much potential for display. Jugs, cups, plates and pots in cheerful colours and patterns delight the eye (overleaf).

circumference, a lower compartment for ledgers and an inset secret compartment for keeping money safe.

Such designs tend to be fairly specific, and it is difficult not to put them to a use similar to that for which they were first intended. For greater flexibility, it may be necessary to borrow ideas from other areas. A cross-over between commercial and domestic use can be amusing and add a great deal of live-liness and interest. Try hanging an old wooden printers' tray on the wall – the little compartments, originally designed to store metal type, can be used to display a col-lection of perfume bottles, spices or pots of artist's colours. Large wicker laundry baskets on castors make ideal toy baskets, or you can fill them full of sports equipment – all the hockey sticks, tennis racquets and cricket bats that usually litter the hall. Old

shop fittings, from drapers', old hardware stores, gentlemen's outfitters and similarly old-fashioned establishments, make surprisingly attractive and versatile storage systems. Wooden pigeonholes, glass-fronted display cases, old wooden filing cabinets and card index files can be adapted to a wide range of uses, from clothes storage to fittings for a study or library.

But for the height of versatility and appropriateness, it is hard to better the country classic – the basket. From fine painted wicker or woven rush, to more rustic twig and vine baskets, there is a style to suit every taste. The standard fireside accompaniment, the log basket, can also be

a handy place to tidy toys. Magazines and newspapers, knitting and sewing materials and even cosmetics can all be kept in baskets. Lloyd Loom basketweave accessories, now increasingly collected, are also very sympathetic. Made of paper-wrapped wire rather than wicker, standard pieces include corner or upright laundry bins as well as blanket boxes.

ON SHOW

Somewhere along the line, 'storage' inevitably becomes 'display'. Part of that 'below stairs' appeal comes from tantalizing displays of useful things, well-kept and neatly in order. Collections of objects are always intriguing; the massed effect has immense impact where the display of a single item would not. In a country interior, this kind of grouping can add a sense of pattern and texture – think of a collection of straw hats hanging on the wall, or half a dozen different baskets suspended from the ceiling. The overall effect is one of a delightful managed clutter, where relatively humble things are given pride of place.

The kitchen, naturally, is the place where storage and display are often indistinguishable. Plate racks filled with country china, cups and mugs hanging from a line of hooks, jelly moulds and dough cutters making a pattern on the wall are all simple and attractive ideas. Elsewhere in the home you can take the same approach, to create vivid still-life arrangements on tabletops, shelves, in glass-fronted cabinets or simply hanging on the wall. What you collect together in one place should have some kind of common characteristic – a textural quality, a colour or a function. The beauty of ordinary things is a fundamental part of the satisfaction of country living.

THE NURSERY

One place where keeping things on view is a sound idea is the nursery. Children hate to see all their toys put away and a nursery devoid of clutter is a pretty soulless place. On the other hand, parents like to think there is some semblance of order behind the nursery door. A compromise is to create an arrangement of reachable shelves or racks where treasures, dolls, stuffed animals, and all the other precious possessions can find a home. Toys always look colourful and

An unusual corner for display has been created by adding rough plank shelves over the old whitewashed construction, making a feature out of a redundant area (left). Blue and white pottery and glass jars have a cool look which complements the chalky finish of the walls. A delicate arrangement of naive carved birds is given importance by its position on top of a lovely carved side table (above right). Dressers combine open display shelves with closed storage drawers or cupboards. This unusual variation on the theme, with an intriguing scalloped trim and rough planked door fronts, provides the opportunity to show off a collection of bold and brightly coloured ceramics (below right).

For toys such as
Lego, bricks,
puzzles or any set with
a million tiny
components, organize
a system of shallow
painted baskets or
wooden boxes which
stack when not in use.
Paint the containers
different colours to
encourage children to
keep games separate.

charming out on view, and it is reassuring to the child to have them within reach. And, at the end of the day, it is always a good idea to have a large hamper, wicker basket or blanket box where the worst of the clutter can be hurled, at least temporarily. The children can be involved, too – this kind of tidying up usually appeals to them, even if just for a while.

Children's rooms or nurseries usually accommodate more than train sets, teddies and jigsaws. If there are two children sharing the room, the younger may still need a changing area, with all the attendant paraphernalia. There will, of course, be the need to store clothes and perhaps bedding; as the children grow, there will be increased demand for study space, room for books and school equipment. Consequently, unless you can afford to redecorate and re-equip the room to cope with each stage of their lives, aim to build a little flexibility into the room design and storage arrangements.

Shelves will always be useful; large baskets or hampers can take sports kits when the toys are outgrown; plain containers will still be acceptable when they are needed for fan magazines and tapes. If you want to impose a little style on what would otherwise be a cheerful disorganization, do it in paint which can be changed easily and cheaply as the children grow. A child's enthusiasm for a cartoon-character wallpaper may be short-lived and the paper then costly to replace. For young children, you might like to add a stencilled pattern or motif to give the room the outward appearance of co-ordination. And you can reinforce the theme with bedding, curtains or blinds.

COUNTRY ENTRANCE HALLS ARE SOMETIMES SEPARATED FROM THE CORRIDOR BEYOND BY A HEAVY CURTAIN, WHICH HELPS TO KEEP IN HEAT AND CREATE A FEELING OF COSINESS. TRY HANGING THICK FABRIC, EVEN KELIMS, OR FILMY LACE OR COTTON FOR TOTALLY DIFFERENT PARTITIONING EFFECTS.

In the past simple country furniture, such as this pine wardrobe, was usually painted, rather than left with a natural finish (above left). The soft tones and delicate flower painting on this piece make it a sympathetic choice for a nursery. Nursery colours do not need to be pale and pastel; here sunshine yellow contrasts with a rich green to make a warm colour scheme (below left). Natural fibre matting laid wall to wall is a practical flooring choice. A dresser flanked with wooden benches makes a flexible and welcoming arrangement in a hallway (above).

THE HALL

Often overlooked and sadly neglected, the hall has an important part to play in the well-tempered household. One important function for it to fulfil is an organizational one. The hall is where you leave and enter the house, where post and parcels arrive, where messages are left, where coats are put on and taken off. But although it is the scene of such busy traffic, it is not a place where people expect to spend much time. For this reason, it can be put to good use as a place for storing outdoor wear and for making an efficient

Buffs, creams, stone, whites and greys are all suitable colours to paint a hall. For a livelier look, simulate a stone effect to emphasize the hall's role as a link with the outside. Neutral shades have another advantage in that they make the perfect background for collections of pictures and prints and other displays.

transition from indoors to out and vice versa.

Traditional hall furniture has a strong appeal of its own. The hallstand incorporating coat hooks, pegs for hats, a drawer for gloves, a mirror, a shelf for letters and parcels and a stand for dripping umbrellas is a classic Victorian piece. Alternatively, you might prefer the more restrained style of a bentwood hat stand. If the hall is big enough, larger pieces of country furniture, such as dressers, chests of drawers or tables can provide room for depositing belongings, for a telephone or for a stack of letters.

Once the hall begins to function as a working space, hub of the comings and goings of the household, it will have a character of its own, and this relates to its second important role, to provide a welcome for guests. A bland corridor looks forbidding. A hall decorated with the same care as the rest of the house is friendly and inviting.

Surfaces will take a great deal of wear and flooring, in particular, needs to be especially practical. Hard floors such as quarry tiles, stone, or black and white ceramic tiles provide excellent solutions. In terms of decoration, the hall is a connecting area, meeting the different colour and pattern schemes of the rooms which lead off it. For this reason, it is often advisable to paint the hall a neutral background shade which will work with all colours.

The hall is a good place for display (above left). Group objects in sympathetic arrangements for greater impact. An antique leather carrying case makes an unusual umbrella stand (below left). If there is the opportunity, it is a good idea to have a display of flowers at the entrance (right).

Mary Emmerling's Weekend Retreat

Author and leading authority on American country style – or, as it is cheerfully known, 'Americana' – Mary Emmerling has her own country retreat, where she and her family and friends spend weekends away from the pressures of New York. Situated in a resort town on Long Island, the retreat actually consists of four little cottages, which started life as fairly basic structures where potato farmers took the sea air. In Mary's hands, the cottages have been transformed into comfortable family homes. Here she can exercise her decorating skills and indulge her love of appealing items from America's past.

Mary's work involves travelling extensively and during the course of these travels she collects all kinds of objects, from old baskets to unusual plates or cutlery that might be useful as props for her books. Increasingly, she is also on the look out for items for clients, who may commission her to assemble a collection of spongeware or

country furniture for their home. Familiar with many out-of-the-way flea markets, auction rooms, junk shops and antique dealers all over the country, Mary has naturally amassed her own collection of favourite finds.

Some people with a bug for collecting simply lock their treasures away, bringing them out, if at all, only for celebrations. Mary's approach could not be more different. To her, storage means display. And anything out on view is more likely to be used and enjoyed every day, not just on special occasions. Linen tablecloths and silverware are not hidden in a drawer, but used often, in a spirit of living for the present.

Much of Mary's storage consists

of open display shelves and peg racks. Plates, platters, glasses, cups and saucers are out on full view, ready to be taken down and used when the need arises. Peg racks make hanging displays of hats, jackets, towels – whatever is appropriate for the room in question. Mary even keeps her collection of turquoise jewellery hanging from hooks in the bathroom: in this way, she is more likely to remember to put it on than if it were languishing in the bottom of a jewellery case.

Baskets, those indispensable country items, hold everything from bathroom accessories to bread and potatoes. In the kitchen, wire baskets are used for root vegetables and fresh corn; another

hanging basket stows utensils for the barbecue. On the big country table is a collection of white pitchers, used for displays of seasonal flowers.

This type of natural abundance goes well with the country mood. Objects are endlessly recycled. Mary pools the resources of the four cottages for large gatherings, changes the emphasis according to the season and constantly rotates what she has, so that nothing is forgotten. A few things, naturally, find a home in cupboards, such as cleaning products and the like. But most of her possessions are out in the open, in the kind of generous display that seems to be particularly synonymous with country style.

CHAPTER THREE

OUTDOOR ROOMS

NATURE IS NEVER FAR AWAY WHEN YOU ARE AT HOME IN THE COUNTRY. FROM THE FRONT DOORWAY FRAMED BY FRAGRANT CLIMBING ROSES OR WISTERIA, YOU GAZE WITH SATISFACTION AT COLOURFUL BORDERS BRIMMING WITH COTTAGE FLOWERS, OR ACROSS A VELVET LAWN SHADED BY BOUNTIFUL OLD FRUIT TREES. FURTHER ON, IN A SECLUDED CORNER UNDER AN ARCH THICK WITH BLOSSOMING HONEYSUCKLE AND CLEMATIS, A LITTLE GARDEN SEAT MAKES THE PERFECT SPOT FOR A QUIET HOUR WITH A GOOD BOOK.

The outdoor room, half garden, half interior, is where nature can be enjoyed in sheltered conditions. The quality of light is very important, not only to encourage growth, but also to create a mood of tranquillity.

Of course, living close to nature is easier if your house is surrounded by an idyllic garden and if your windows overlook rolling hills and green fields. But there are many ways of bringing a sense of the outdoors into the home even if its location is far from ideal. With careful planning, and careful planting, the house and its activities can seem to flow into the garden and almost merge with it.

MAKING AN ENTRANCE

Just as the hall sets the tone and character for the rest of the house, the main entrance also creates a lasting impression for everyone on first arrival. In the country, the impression you want to create is that of a house perfectly at ease with its surroundings, and blending naturally with them.

Planting which softens the lines of the house and frames doors and windows helps to anchor the house visually in its setting. Every country cottage, it seems, must have roses growing over the door. In fact, most climbers are an excellent way of achieving this effect, their rambling growth providing a green veil to soften brickwork and other hard materials. With many species there is the added bonus of abundant flowers and scent. As so often in the garden, the traditional favourites – in this case honeysuckle, wisteria, jasmine and climbing or rambling old-fashioned roses – are hard to beat.

A certain care must be exercised when choosing climbers, however. A few species, such as some ivies, are very invasive and will literally wrench the mortar from the brickwork as they attach themselves to the façade. Very prolific growers can also hold

pitfalls for the unwary: Russian vine (*Polygonum baldschuanicum*) for instance, is quick to smother everything in its path, which may be an advantage when you want to disguise an eyesore but is not so appropriate for enhancing the front of your house. Size and maintenance need to be borne in mind, too. Wisterias, for instance, spectacular as they are, need to be pruned twice a year and will grow to an enormous size. Another consideration is a plant's appearance in winter. There's no hiding a climber which wreathes the front door, so it might be worth looking out for varieties which are evergreen in order to avoid having to look at bare stems for months on end. This is the obvious advantage of ivies, of course, but other evergreen climbers are not hard to find. The lovely Japanese honeysuckle (*Lonicera japonica* 'Halliana') keeps its leaves in all but the coldest winters, and bears its clusters of fragrant white and pale yellow flowers from June well into the autumn. *Magnolia grandiflora* makes a stately though slow-growing evergreen wall shrub, with the bonus of large and deliciously scented creamy white

A porch or veranda is a traditional outdoor room in many parts of the world, somewhere cool to sit on warm evenings (right). In very hot countries, it is important to protect doorways from the effects of blazing sun (far right, above). Here a thick canopy of vines filters the light and a fine muslin curtain acts as a screen. Roses growing over the door sum up the appeal of the country cottage, smothering the entrance in colour and scent (far right, below).

flowers from July to September. The most reliable evergreen clematis is *C. armandii,* studded with sweet-smelling white flowers in April, while *C. florida,* which bears white flowers in early summer, is semi-evergreen. And of the roses *R.* 'Mermaid' is not only extremely vigorous and covered in huge creamy yellow scented blooms in summer, but it is also virtually evergreen. Certain clematis will also tolerate being grown in containers. Many climbers, including jasmine, most varieties of clematis and roses, need to be supported, either with wires or on trellises. Small fruit trees can also be espaliered against a wall.

Flower colour is also something to consider. Roses in delicate pinks and whites complement pale stone (the silvery pink 'New Dawn' and palest cream 'Mme Alfred Carrière' are both scented and vigorous); while the blue-grey flowers of wisteria are beautiful against mellow brickwork (though as wisteria is slow to mature, you may have to wait some years for the full effect). For sheer drama it is hard to beat Virginia creeper (*Parthenocissus quinquefolia*). This self-climber actually protects brickwork and makes a dense cover for any wall. In the autumn the leaves turn flame-red in a short-lived but dazzling display.

THE CONSERVATORY

The true conservatory, a Victorian in-spiration, is a splendid place. New tech-nology in the nineteenth century, par-ticularly in the fields of structural ironwork and glass manufacture, conspired to fulfil the Victorian dream of growing exotic tender species year-round. Few really substantial

A skylight and a hanging plant turn any room into an outdoor room, where natural light and a feeling of connection with the outdoors can be enjoyed (above left). A kitchen built on to the outside of a house has the feeling of an outdoor room, with large plants, lots of light and simple, slightly battered furniture (below left). Cane blinds pull across the glass roof of this sunroom to cut out the brightest light and make the room more pleasant to live in (above). Cane or wicker furniture is a natural choice for any outdoor room.

Victorian houses were without a lacy confection of white-painted ironwork supporting intricate patterns of glass panels, densely planted with luxuriant ferns, palms and various tropical species.

What we understand by a conservatory today may range from such a glorious original design right through to a simple sunny corner top-lit by a glass roof. Every household, especially in northern climates, can really benefit from having a relaxing place where a degree of natural warmth allows indoor plants to flourish. Even on grey winter days, this is a place where you can

IDEAS FOR INDIVIDUAL CONSERVATORY PIECES INCLUDE: SIMPLE METAL GARDEN FURNITURE, SUCH AS THE CLASSIC FRENCH PARK CHAIR IN SLATTED WOOD AND METAL; A HAMMOCK AND SOME STRIPED CANVAS DECKCHAIRS; FOR A MORE CONTEMPORARY LOOK, A COLLECTION OF PLAIN CANVAS DIRECTOR'S CHAIRS.

create the illusion of living right in the midst of the garden.

The Victorian taste for exotica was expressed in the style, planting and furnishing of their conservatories, which displayed a delightful jumble of influences from Africa, India and every corner of the empire. Many off-the-peg conservatories produced today are ideal for re-creating this look. A wide range of traditional designs is available in different sizes and to suit different locations. Alternatively you can design and build your own glazed extension, or simply glass in a porch to make a simple sunroom. Whether you are choosing a ready-made conservatory, or dreaming up your own version, it should be in keeping with the architectural style of your house.

The type and density of conservatory planting will depend partly on how much of a living area it is going to be. A true plant enthusiast may wish to devote most of the space to deep contained beds for raising hot-house specimens, or else create a dense jungle atmosphere with vines, ferns and palms. For most of us, however, the real reason for having a conservatory has less to do with horticulture than with relaxation. A few permanent plants such as container-grown climbers, large potted ferns or palms, together with large house-plants such as weeping fig will provide a basic framework to which can be added other container plants set out on built-in ledges or metal staging. Arrange the planting in the same way as you would any garden design, with contrasts of leaf shape, variations in height and spread and lively splashes of colour.

After the planting is established you can get on with the fun of furnishing the conservatory. First there are a few practical considerations to bear in mind. In any glazed area that is filled with a dense concentration

A conservatory can be a room where one can literally sit in the garden, separated only by glass from the natural world outside. Here the furnishings are deliberately simple and pale, to keep attention focused on the view (left). The grey-green colour of the framework of this garden room is carried through in the colour of the chairs and wooden cupboard which furnish it (right).

of plants there will be a fair amount of humidity. Whatever furniture you choose must be able to withstand exposure to moist, warm air, as well as strong sunlight. Fine wood finishes or expensive printed fabrics will quickly deteriorate under such conditions. Instead, like the Victorians, borrow furnishing styles from the tropics. Lightweight garden furniture in rattan, bamboo and wickerwork makes classic conservatory pieces. There are many acceptable examples of basketwork furniture produced today, but it is more effective and enjoyable to collect your own original discoveries. You can still find good Victorian and Edwardian designs in second-hand shops, as well as Lloyd Loom pieces from this century. A collection of slightly different chairs and tables, all painted in a single shade to give unity, makes a charming conservatory collection. Pale mint green, cream, yellow and ice blue are excellent colours for furniture, and look delightful against a background of dark green foliage.

A conservatory is not the place for much in the way of soft furnishing. The floor will be hard and waterproof and finishes generally need to be robust. But comfort is still important and can be supplied in the form of cushions or loose covers which can be removed easily for cleaning or renewal. For the right combination of informality and practicality, choose heavy plain cotton drill, ticking, gingham or old chintz in soft and faded shades. Pad the seats of wickerwork or metal furniture with deep cushions, transform an old sofa by throwing a plain cotton loose cover over it, and add squab cushions to café chairs.

Although in general the conservatory should be underfurnished, here as in any other room details and finishing touches can make all the difference. Pictures and paintings are out of the question, but an old mirror in an attractively weathered gilt frame can add a decorative flourish as well as maximizing light. A lichen-encrusted garden statue half-hidden in the undergrowth is also in keeping with the overall ambience. For a more rustic look, arrange a collection of terracotta pots or bold ceramic urns in a corner or on a ledge.

An outdoor eating area, set up under the shelter of a flourishing vine, is particularly inviting (above). The whitewashed walls and white furniture are complemented by white flowers. Bright colours look good under a strong sun and painted wooden furniture is a feature of many Mediterranean areas (above right). Eating under direct sun can be uncomfortable (below right). This canopy of split cane is a delightful screen.

ON THE TERRACE

The equivalent outdoor space to the conservatory is the terrace or patio. Here is another opportunity to blend house and garden, dissolving boundaries and creating an enjoyable extension of living space.

If you have the opportunity to site a new terrace, consider the aspect with great care. Some compromise may be necessary, especially if the sunniest position is on a blank side of the house, where there is no access, or the living areas indoors connect with a part of the garden perpetually in shade

or exposed to wind. With luck you will be able to create a terrace which can be reached easily from either living room, conservatory, dining-room or kitchen, but still benefits from good light and wind conditions. If you are able to widen the access to the terrace, by putting in French windows for example, you will emphasize its role as a natural extension of the house.

You can also give a terrace added impact by building in a change of level, so that you look down on the garden, or up to it if the terrace is sunken. Bear in mind, too, that the shape of the terrace should reflect the basic garden design. A terrace which ends in a curve will complement the sweep of curved beds, whereas a rectangular or square design

is more in keeping with the regularity of long straight borders.

Materials for a terrace should be as natural as possible. Reclaimed frostproof brick, York stone, wooden decking and granite setts all weather beautifully and last for ever. York stone in particular, however, is very expensive.

If the terrace is to function as an outdoor room, you will have to give some thought to furnishing. As in the conservatory, plain, robust styles are more appropriate for chairs and tables than the fussier reproduction wrought-ironwork or synthetic garden furniture. Simple designs in wood, either painted or treated with preservative, will weather sympathetically and go well with

IF YOU CHOOSE AN ARTIFICIAL MATERIAL FOR YOUR TERRACE, TRY TO LEAVE ROOM FOR GROWING LITTLE CLUMPS OF CUSHIONING PLANTS, SUCH AS THYME, DIANTHUS OR HELIANTHEMUM, TO GIVE THE 'STONE' A MORE NATURAL APPEARANCE. YOU CAN ALSO ENCOURAGE THE GROWTH OF LICHENS BY PAINTING THE SURFACE WITH UNPASTEURIZED MILK.

A terrace can be a transitional place between the house and garden (far left). Here a climber, trained up the porch supports, frames the entrance to the garden, creating a setting where it is pleasant to pause and relax. A terracotta pot on a black plinth gives a sunken terrace a classical feel (left). Deckchairs in the sun make the most of a sunny spot; a white lace cloth instantly dresses an outdoor table and adds a cool note (above).

any architectural or garden style. Folding park chairs, canvas deckchairs, director's chairs and even wickerwork pieces are all light enough to be assembled at a moment's notice, brought out from the shed or from the conservatory and taken back in at night or if it starts to rain. In the same way, cushions can be brought out on to the terrace to make built-in stone benches or metal seats more comfortable.

If the terrace is in a sunny position you will probably need to organize some form of shading, especially if you intend to eat outdoors. A climber or vine can be trained over a simple wooden framework to give the dappled shade that is so pleasant on a hot, bright day. If the light is particularly strong, you might need the greater protection of a canvas awning. And for sitting outside under the stars enjoying a nightcap, it is worth going to the trouble of fitting some form of discreet outdoor lighting to lend a little drama to the planting.

Rosemary Verey's Garden Room

When it comes to the design of a conservatory or garden room, most people naturally think in terms of the lacy wrought-iron constructions popular in the nineteenth century. But for this extension to a small house, which was originally converted from a seventeenth-century stable block, a Victorian or Edwardian style would have been quite unsympathetic. Instead, the new garden room was designed in a classical manner, its elegant, graceful proportions and relatively restrained detailing perfectly in keeping with the setting.

When gardener and writer Rosemary Verey moved here from a much larger house three years ago, she felt the need for extra space, somewhere pleasant where visitors could sit in the summer and which could also serve as a winter home for tender plants. She consulted Norfolk architect Charles Morris, who came up with a design to build a garden room directly adjoining the drawing room. The new extension faces southeast and leads out onto a sheltered paved area.

Altogether, the new room resembles a loggia rather than an enclosed structure, light and airy

linking three small pools. In the topmost pool are goldfish, reflected in an overhead mirror. The grotto evolved as a solution to the problem of what to do about a permanently damp section of wall.

Aside from the grotto, the garden room is very simply furnished. The floor is a combination of dressed stone flags and local maltings tiles. Furniture comes from Rosemary's previous drawing room and kitchen. The fabric used to cover both the table and armchairs has a suitable 'climbing geranium' pattern.

This simplicity of decoration allows the emphasis to fall on the plants, a mixture of permanent planting and plants in pots. Permanent residents include arum lilies, which flower for a long period, plumbago and *Cobaea scandens* (cup and saucer creeper), which is constantly covered in purple bell flowers. But by far the greater number of plants are in pots to allow flexibility of arrangement, and many of these are scented leaf geraniums. Rosemary, who enjoys scented plants and scented leaf geraniums in particular, is a firm believer in growing what one really likes.

Emphatically not a sun room, but a room for plants, this garden room is the next best thing to the outdoors for someone who prefers outdoors to in.

despite its solidity. Woodwork is painted a dark green: white would have been too bright and obvious, and would have drawn too much attention away from the stone-work and the domed glass roof.

Inside, half-concealed amid the profusion of plants, is an enchanting surprise. A grotto, constructed of abalone and mussel shells, coral and vermiculated stone, supports a tiny waterfall

CONTAINERS

The terrace is the place for putting all your
ideas about container gardening into
practice. There is a huge variety of plant
containers on the market, which can be supplemented by an equal number of 'found'
containers adapted from other sources.
Again, natural materials look best, age well
and are generally more in keeping with the
landscape than containers made of plastic,
concrete or similar. It is definitely worth the
extra expense.

Wooden containers, either painted or
treated with preservative, are fairly economical and can also be easy to make. Proper
Versailles tubs need not look too formal,
especially if planted with small fruit trees or
bushes rather than clipped standards. Large
rectangular wooden boxes like oversized
window boxes make inconspicuous but
highly versatile planters. Old stone troughs
or sinks contribute the important dimension
of texture; terracotta bowls look superb
filled with spring bulbs, and the classic lines
of a stone urn provide an elegant focal point.

There is also room in even the most
serious garden design for the odd playful
touch. Pails, tin baths, watering cans,
chimney pots, and old wheelbarrows contribute a sense of fun and surprise.

The secret of container gardening is to
adopt a wholehearted approach. Group pots
and containers in impressive arrays – don't
dot them about where their impact will be
lost. Remember that if they are in full sun
they will need watering at least once a day
in summer. Regular feeding is important
too. The containers themselves should also
be large enough to retain moisture and to be

A stone sink is the ideal container for a herb and alpine garden (left). Cheerful ivy-leaved pelargoniums in pots flank the terrace, adding colour and height. A striking colour contrast makes an entrance more dramatic. The deep blue door is accented by pink pelargoniums (above).

ANY CONTAINER CAN BE USED TO GROW PLANTS AS LONG AS IT HOLDS ENOUGH COMPOST, DRAINS FREELY AND IS STABLE. IF NECESSARY, IT CAN BE LINED WITH BLACK PLASTIC SHEETING WHICH THE PLANT GROWTH WILL THEN CONCEAL. FOLLOW THE COUNTRY SPIRIT OF IMPROVISATION AND PLANT UP COLANDERS AND CHIMNEY POTS, GALVANIZED BUCKETS AND RUSTIC WIRE BASKETS.

worthy of attention – scale is important. Finally, they should be filled to abundance, not planted with a few straggling specimens.

A surprising range of plants adapt well to container life, and some positively flourish. You can grow herbs, vegetables and even fruit trees as well. In a shady corner you could set pots of ferns, hostas and trailing ivy. Impatiens, azaleas and petunias all provide valuable colour. Many flowering shrubs, such as lacecap or mophead hydrangeas, azaleas and many others, can do well in containers if well watered; pansies and forget-me-nots can be planted under bushier varieties. Foliage plants such as fragrant lemon balm contribute interest through leaf shape and form. And spring bulbs are perfect container plants, ushering in the growing season.

When positioning containers, exploit any changes in level, such as steps or ledges. Container plants also make an attractive sight at an entrance. In the country, plants that are naturally abundant are more at home than those with neat growing habits. The classic pair of bay trees in Versailles tubs is perhaps just a little too formal, for example, and more reminiscent of the Georgian town square than the country village. Clipped

box, however, especially in whimsical shapes of animals or birds, is strong on character and period atmosphere.

Scent is also important. Bushy lavender can be very effective grown in containers. Its delicate flower spikes will attract bees and produce a delightful scent to drift in through open windows. The 'Hidcote' variety is compact in shape and has vivid purple-blue flowers. Aromatic thyme, rosemary, bay, sage and lemon-scented verbena (*Lippia citriodora*) will also all grow happily in pots. Other sweet-scented shrubs, more suitable for beds than containers, include varieties of philadelphus (mock orange) viburnum, Mexican orange blossom (*Choisya ternata*), witch hazel (*Hamamelis mollis*) and skimmia.

Hanging baskets filled with annuals in paintbox shades are a perennial feature of country exteriors: in fact they may have become a little too popular, and are now more suggestive of the public house than the private house. For a change of look, try filling a basket with trailing herbs or foliage plants in soft greys and greens, such as silvery helichrysums and variegated ivies, rather than the standard lobelia and pelargoniums.

Window boxes are versatile containers for virtually any location. They can look particularly effective filled with a single variety or colour, such as the nodding yellow heads

A charming group of different containers frames a doorway overlooked by a scarecrow (left). Baskets, pots and bowls have been chosen to suit the type of plant, its size and habit of growth. The restrained classicism of this terracotta container is the perfect foil for the splash of bright red dahlias (above right).

GOOD PLANTS TO GROW FOR FOLIAGE INCLUDE: HOSTAS, HOLLY AND IVY; COTTON LAVENDER FOR GREY–GREEN LEAVES; EUONYMOUS, ELAEAGNUS AND BERGENIA YEAR-ROUND. IN THE WINTER BRIGHT RED DOGWOOD STEMS MAKE STUNNING DISPLAYS, AS DO PYRACANTHA OR COTONEASTER BRANCHES LADEN WITH FLAME–RED BERRIES.

of daffodils in spring. Changing window-box planting is a quick and easy way of responding to the seasons, which in turn makes your house seem even more closely tied to its setting. At the same time, it provides an instant facelift for the exterior.

GARDEN PRODUCE

As well as creating indoor/outdoor spaces within the house and without, making use of what you actually grow in the garden is deeply satisfying. Every garden is capable of producing at least some flowers for cutting, a few herbs for cooking and a selection of vegetable and fruit crops.

The ideal, of course, is to have enough land to include several gardens within its boundary. First, there should be a walled kitchen garden, laid out in neat rows and well stocked with vegetable and salad crops.

Then there should be a herb garden, perhaps in a traditional Elizabethan knot design, supplying a whole range of herbs for cooking and medicinal purposes. Deep herbaceous borders would supply a wealth of blooms for all the flower arrangements in the house. Beyond the flower garden there would be a wild flower meadow and an orchard of fruit trees. And in a distant corner, a beehive would produce nectar subtly flavoured by all the wild flowers and blossom.

Every gardener's dream, perhaps, but there are many ways of adapting these ideas to gardens on a much smaller scale, which can give you at least some of the pleasure of growing your own produce. Herbs, for example, flourish in pots and a collection of container herbs in a sunny corner of the terrace or on a window sill can supply enough flavouring to meet many of your culinary needs. Herbs tend to have distinctive-looking foliage which can also add a more decorative dimension. Borders edged with chives, clumps of low-growing thyme, crinkly parsley or the silver grey spikes of rosemary combine beauty with usefulness. Some fruit trees, notably cherry, pear and apple, also accept being grown in tubs; and strawberries in special strawberry pots make a charming and fruitful addition to any garden scheme.

When space is limited, copy the traditional cottage garden notion and grow vegetables in among the flowers. The scarlet flowers of runner beans, ornamental varieties of cabbage, lettuce and endive, the feathery leaves of young carrots and the sheen of ripe tomatoes are delightful and decorative enough to grace any herbaceous border.

MOST HERBS DO WELL IN CONTAINERS. CHIVES WILL FLOURISH IN A WINDOW BOX. BASIL, PARSLEY AND CORIANDER – WHICH ARE ALL ANNUALS – CAN BE SOWN IN POTS EVERY YEAR. SAGE, ROSEMARY AND THYME ARE PERENNIALS AND LOVE A SUNNY POSITION. MINT SHOULD DEFINITELY BE GROWN IN A POT OR CONTAINER – UNLESS YOU WANT IT TO TAKE OVER THE GARDEN!

This outdoor eating area is composed of a simple wooden table and canvas chairs – a far cry from over-elaborate or synthetic garden furniture (left). In an outdoor area, finishes are more attractive when they are weathered and worn. This delightful table is a case in point (above).

Planning a garden to supply flowers for indoor arrangements means ensuring a year-round supply of foliage, stems and interesting seedheads or fruits to substitute for or supplement the blooms. Flowers which are indispensable for cutting and which also make excellent border plants include the hardy chrysanthemum and the marguerite, the versatile and lovely columbine, or aquilegia, dianthus, primroses and hellebores for spring arrangements and scabious, a valuable source of blue in summer displays.

75

PICK FLOWERS FIRST THING IN THE MORNING OR AT THE END OF THE DAY. AVOID DAMAGED OR DISCOLOURED FLOWERS, STEMS OR LEAVES AND CHOOSE FLOWERS THAT ARE BEGINNING TO OPEN UP RATHER THAN THOSE IN FULL BLOOM OR TIGHT BUD. AS SOON AS YOU HAVE CUT THEM, PUT THE FLOWERS STRAIGHT INTO DEEP COOL WATER FOR SEVERAL HOURS.

Sedums, with their dark pinky-red heads and broad leaves are very useful for the flower arranger in autumn. The sharp greeny yellow flowers of *Alchemilla mollis* add a vibrant accent to almost any combination. And, in every country garden, there is room for at least one variety of old rose.

Winter is inevitably the least productive time. Aside from hellebores and the delicate yellow stars of winter-flowering jasmine, you may have to rely on material you have dried from the previous summer or autumn.

Finally, try to set aside some space in your garden for encouraging wildlife and insects. An unmown patch of grass under some trees, seeded with wild flowers, may not be directly productive in terms of crops or cut flowers but it will make a valuable ecological contribution and help sustain nature in its broadest sense.

Lavender edging a pathway makes a wonderful scented walk. Lavender is invaluable: it has a delightful scent, which it retains even when dried, and can be put to countless culinary and household uses.

LIVING IN THE GARDEN

As an extension of the idea of an outdoor room, you can create little enclaves in the garden where you can sit, read, enjoy a drink or simply contemplate the joys of nature. Such retreats – whether half-hidden or in full view – are the focal points of good garden design. A stone bench set into a shrubbery, a summerhouse just visible at the bottom of an orchard, a weathered tree seat encircling an old oak, or a scented walkway under an arch of rambling roses will entice you into the garden again and again to appreciate and savour its beauty.

Sir Roy Strong's Gothick Arbour

Sir Roy Strong, former director of the National Portrait Gallery and the Victoria and Albert Museum, is passionate about gardening. It was during his tenure at the V & A that he first saw the structure which has become one of the favourite sitting places in his Herefordshire garden.

In 1979, the year in which Sir Roy staged 'The Garden', an exhibition commemorating one thousand years of British gardening, he saw this Gothick arbour by Francis Machyn at the Chelsea Flower Show. It captivated Sir Roy and he was photographed in it to illustrate a newspaper article. His first impressions were confirmed and he knew he had to acquire one for the garden which he and his wife were creating in the country.

Like many such purchases, the arbour was intended for one particular spot but ended up somewhere quite different. Now it sits at the end of an avenue, looking out over daffodils in spring which give way in early summer to white Queen Anne's lace and clumps of allium. Painted light grey – as Sir Roy believes that white is too brash for the garden – the arbour faces west and has *Clematis tangutica* growing on one side, and

Dutch honeysuckle on the other.

Sir Roy's garden is very large; the arbour is one of a number of sitting places which offer vantage points from which to admire the planting. Another is in the rose garden, where grey-leaved plants like artemisia and senecio create a

foil for the pale, subtle colours of old roses. Here Sir Roy has a stone bench, flanked by two cherub warriors, all, surprisingly, in reconstituted stone but given the patina of age by liberal anointings with sour milk, which encourages the growth of algae and lichens.

The size of the garden, and the Strongs' ambitions for it, do not permit much in the way of idle sitting in arbours. But they make sure that they do set aside some time just to chat, have tea or, on warm summer evenings, a glass of wine, and enjoy looking at the fruits of their labours. When they have friends to stay, they take a basket filled with a bottle, glasses and tea towel and repair to the arbour for drinks. For Sir Roy, such moments are ones of pure happiness: he recommends that everyone with a garden should also have a place where they can sit and enjoy it.

CHAPTER FOUR

A BREAK FOR LUNCH

THE COUNTRY DINING-ROOM IS ONE OF THE GREAT CONVIVIAL GATHERING PLACES. THE SCENE OF QUIET COMPANIONABLE LUNCHES, RIOTOUS FAMILY GET-TOGETHERS, OR EVERYDAY MEALTIMES, IT IS A STAGE SET FOR EATING. AS A CELEBRATION OF HOME COOKING, FRESH PRODUCE AND GOOD COMPANY, IT IS VERY FAR FROM THE SOLEMN, FORMAL AND LIFELESS DINING-ROOMS COMMON A CENTURY AGO. THE SPIRIT OF COUNTRY INFORMALITY HAS CAUGHT ON EVERYWHERE.

Warm yellow washed walls are set off by blue-grey woodwork and a whitewashed beamed ceiling in this country kitchen. An old table covered with a checked oilcloth provides room for informal lunches – a cheerful, homely setting.

MATERIALS ARE NATURAL AND UNCONTRIVED, the decor welcoming and warm, and the activities of the rest of the house are not excluded but positively encouraged to spill over and enliven what might otherwise be redundant space for long periods of the day. What better place to meet over a bowl of homemade soup, a chunk of fresh crusty bread and a glass of wine?

ORIGINAL KITCHEN DRESSERS CAN BE VERY EXPENSIVE. MAKE YOUR OWN INSTEAD, BY PUTTING AN OLD BOOKCASE OR SOME WOODEN SHELVING TOGETHER WITH A BASE CONSISTING OF A JUNKSHOP CUPBOARD OR CHEST. FIX THE SHELVING TO THE WALL AND SLOT THE CUPBOARD UNDERNEATH OR REST THE SHELVING ON TOP. THEN PAINT BOTH PARTS THE SAME COLOUR, DISTRESSING THE FINISH IF YOU WISH.

A MOVABLE FEAST

Maintaining a special room devoted solely to dining is increasingly a luxury in these space-conscious times. In the country, there is ample precedent for setting up eating areas within rooms which principally serve other functions. Naturally the first choice is the kitchen. Large light kitchens with room to spare easily accommodate a family dining

It is important, then, that a conducive spot is found for this midday gathering. Cold, uninspiring corners are unlikely to make everyone want to leave what they are doing and flock around the lunch table. The first decision to be made is where this spot will be – within another room such as the kitchen or living room, or in an area created specifically for this purpose.

A truly splendid array of shelves filled with crockery, jugs and mugs creates the effect of a huge dresser, providing a decorative background for this kitchen dining area (above). For the cook, it is a quick, convenient step from hob or sink to table. A wide, ancient hearth fitted with a stove and flue is the natural focal point in this dining-room (right). Comfortable armchairs make this a room for eating and relaxing.

area. This is a practical notion for all sorts of reasons. The cook can keep an eye on proceedings at both the stove and the table, adjudicate in the odd squabble between junior family members, mop up spills and dispense second helpings. Surfaces and finishes in the kitchen are invariably wipable, washable and reasonably robust, which means that mealtimes can be free of the

anxiety that can ensue when a toddler, a beaker of juice and a fine carpet or mahogany table get acquainted.

From the cook's point of view, it is handy to have an extra work surface free between meals for preparing vegetables, rolling pastry, or any other space-consuming activity. The kitchen table also makes a convenient focus for family and friends as they drift in and out of the kitchen, read the paper, do their homework or just pull up a chair and have a chat. The innate warmth and vitality of a kitchen eating area quickly establishes it as the heart of the house.

Living rooms can also offer space for dining areas. L-shaped living rooms naturally divide in two, as do front and back parlours connected with an arch or double doors. But provided there is enough space, all you have to do to define a dining area is set up a table and chairs. This arrangement works best when there is an easy route between the kitchen and the dining table, either via a connecting door or a hatch. It can also be a real bonus if there is some proximity or access to a terrace for eating outdoors in sunny weather. When the food has been cleared away, the table can be used for any one of a number of activities, such as sewing, homework, playing cards, or doing jigsaw puzzles.

Less conventionally, a dining area can be tucked into a number of other places around the home. In older country houses, the hall may well be fairly substantial in size, big

GOOD CULINARY COMPANIONS INCLUDE:

BASIL – TOMATO, MEAT SAUCES, MUSHROOMS

DILL – FISH, SEAFOOD, SALAD

TARRAGON – CHICKEN, FISH, MAYONNAISE, EGG, TOMATO

MINT – FRESH FRUIT, YOGHURT, LAMB

JUNIPER – GAME, PORK

CHIVES – EGGS, FISH, SALAD

THYME – FISH, BEEF, CHICKEN

FENNEL – FISH, LAMB, SEAFOOD

ROSEMARY – LAMB, CHICKEN, FISH

Outdoor eating should be arranged with as much care as more permanent settings indoors. Cheerful red and green Provençal table linen picks up on the colour of the fresh produce – radishes and tomatoes – to make a delightful outdoor table setting (above right). A butter-yellow embroidered cloth, yellow painted chairs and crockery create a bright, fresh look based on a simple colour theme (below right). Metal baskets and stands complement the curved green metal table and folding chairs in this terrace dining area (far right).

enough to take a drop-leaf table and a few chairs. It may seem odd to eat in a hallway, but provided there is enough space to sit comfortably at table, and access to the kitchen is easy, it can be just as good a place as any other.

Conservatories, sunrooms, porches and terraces often double up as eating areas. In pleasant weather, eating outdoors is irresistible. If you can, follow the sun around the garden. An east-facing spot will catch the early morning sun at breakfast; a south-facing terrace is perfect for a leisurely lunch; and you can move the tea table or deckchairs to a west-facing location to soak up the last rays of the evening sun.

If you are fortunate enough to have the space for a separate dining-room, you may still wish to tempt people into the room at times other than mealtimes just to give it an atmosphere which is warm and lived-in. Dining-rooms can usefully double up as quiet study areas, places to write letters or read.

DECOR FOR DINING

The dining-rooms of the past tended to be rather strongly coloured and dark. A deep green was popular up to the nineteenth century, as was dark panelling. Crimson flock was a more typical Victorian wall covering, striking the appropriate note of opulence and solemnity, especially when combined with engravings of worthy subjects and heavy mahogany furniture.

Our taste today is for rooms which are light and warm, and which serve as a setting for a meal but do not overwhelm it. But this is not to say that they cannot be coloured or patterned as well.

Family eating areas are going to be used throughout the day, not just in the evening, so it is important to choose colours that look good in natural light. A sunny yellow is a typical French country dining-room colour; in the same family of shades are cream, primrose, ivory and buttermilk. For slightly more warmth, you might like to try an ochre wash, pale terracotta, shades of peach or apricot. Sealed but unpainted plaster has a wonderfully warm colour which is intriguing without being insistent. Subtle paint effects, such as colourwashing or glazing, are good at conveying movement and vitality without too overt a patterning. In the cooler spectrum, subtle greys, grey-greens and grey-blues can also be very effective. Eau-de-nil, celadon and pale aquamarine are stylish and restful. Cooler colours, reminiscent of Scandinavian farmhouses, have the effect of intensifying brighter shades and so make good backgrounds for food and table settings.

Aside from painting walls, there are other options which are both practical and decoratively effective. For a family eating room, surfaces and finishes should not be too precious or hard to clean. Tiled and panelled walls both fit the bill. You can half-panel a dining-room with matchboarding up to chair-rail height, or even suggest the effect of panelling with narrow strips of wood applied in a grid all over the wall. Paper borders, stencilled friezes and painted banding are other ways of simulating a panelled effect. And there's no reason why the walls can't be papered, although the choice of pattern is critical. Subtle natural prints, such as those which William Morris

The mellow scene of winter dining, a plain refectory table is set up in front of a deep wide hearth (left). Old country chairs, the plain tiled floor and a deeply recessed window uncovered by curtains or blinds keep the look simple and uncluttered. A warm brick red was chosen for the woodwork to complement the warm tones of the floor. Dining-rooms can double up as areas for work, reading or other activities between mealtimes. As here, it is a simple matter to roll back the tablecloth and use the table as a desk (above). Fresh flowers and bowls of fruit on the table keep the dining area looking lived-in and welcoming.

papers often display, ensure that your attention stays on the food.

Too much fabric in a dining-room, especially in the form of elaborate window drapery, can hold the stale smells of food and tobacco. In any case, there is rarely an absolute requirement for privacy or total screening of light, so simple window treatments are perfectly acceptable. Light muslin curtains, checked gingham or a plain slubbed weave all make good solutions. Since curtains will only be drawn in the evening they can be a stronger colour or a more intense pattern to give a sense of richness under artificial light. Plain roller blinds, crisply pleated Roman blinds, and blinds in natural materials such as slatted wood or cane are also good choices, permitting light control so that brilliant sun does not blind you at the lunch table. And it is always important to bear in mind that if the window has fine

Ideally positioned in front of the hearth, but within sight of the terrace, this dining area benefits from warmth in the winter, a breeze in the summer and natural light all year round (above left). The outdoor eating area is shaded by a canopy of canisse, split bamboo matting common in Mediterranean countries. Strong hot sunlight overhead can make outdoor lunches uncomfortable without some means of shading; canisse is ideal because it filters the light without blocking it completely. An antique wall cabinet, with scalloped edges, makes an attractive place to display glassware (above). A collection of mismatched but harmonious antique chairs are ranged around the walls of this dining-room when not in use. Subtle blue-grey rubbed on the walls makes a sympathetic background to the warm wood tones. Kitchen or dining-room windows often need only the simplest of curtains. Gingham is a natural country choice and always looks fresh and charming (right).

WINDOWS ARE A REAL FOCAL POINT IN A ROOM AND FABRICS ARE NOT THE ONLY FORM OF DRESSING TO CONSIDER. FRAME THE OUTLINE OF A WINDOW WITH A DECORATIVE COLLECTION; ARRANGE GLASS OBJECTS ON THE MIDDLE LEDGE OF A SASH WINDOW SO THEY WILL FILTER THE LIGHT; OR TRAIN A CLIMBING PLANT UP AND OVER THE EDGES OF THE GLASS.

or simply stained a colour. For a slightly softer surface, coir, sisal or other natural fibre matting can be laid, like a carpet, wall to wall. These woven fibres now come in a range of colours and patterns but still have an essentially country feel.

Hard floors, even in natural materials, do have their drawbacks. While they are generally easy to clean and maintain, they are also cold and noisy. And quarry tiles can be particularly unforgiving: whatever you drop will break. It may well be necessary to work out some kind of compromise by combining types of flooring – lay renewable rush matting over quarries, for example, or washable rag rugs over bare wooden boards. Some cotton dhurries can be thrown in the washing machine and these too can deaden the uncomfortable sound of chairs scraping over hard floor.

As in other rooms in the country home, natural finishes are a real advantage. If there are exposed beams, an unplastered brick wall or a bare stone hearth, leave well alone and play up the rusticity. At the most, a thin coat of whitewash is all that's needed.

SETTING THE STAGE

Once the basic surfaces and finishes are taken care of, you can begin to think about furnishing. The Victorians stuffed their dining-rooms full of furniture – sideboards, china cabinets, chiffoniers, and of course table and chairs, all, as often as not, in highly polished mahogany. But the last thing you want to feel in a dining-room is the sense of oppression and claustrophobia that such an arrangement would provoke. All you really need is a table big enough to suit your needs

RAG RUGS WERE TRADITIONALLY MADE FROM COLOURFUL SCRAPS OF OLD CLOTHING AND MATERIAL, KEPT ASIDE SPECIFICALLY FOR THIS PURPOSE. THE STRIPS OF FABRIC WERE USUALLY HOOKED THROUGH A CANVAS BACKING.

details such as working shutters, an unusual shape or strong period character, there is no real reason why it should be covered at all.

What goes underfoot – or under the table – in the dining-room is another key issue. Unless you are absolutely devoted to the idea of carpeting, for practical reasons it is really best avoided. And a family eating area is no place for a treasured oriental rug. Country floors are hard and serviceable, but they need not be unattractive. The mellow surface of old worn quarry tiles, wide polished wooden boards, crisp black and white tiling and stone flags are all full of character. Wooden floors can be painted in a checkered design, stencilled with borders or folk motifs and a selection of comfortable chairs. Whatever else you add should earn its keep, either by serving a useful purpose or contributing a sense of country charm and style.

The dining table is the focal point of the entire room; it's really what the room is all about. What you don't want in a family eating area is a precious antique or in fact any highly polished fine wood surface. Opt instead for the homespun look of scrubbed pine, pale weathered oak or a similarly robust piece which will not only stand up to the occasional spill, but will also provide a practical surface for other activities outside mealtimes. Long refectory tables have a forthright charm, round pedestal tables fit into a bay window or kitchen alcove. There are many original farm or kitchen tables to be had in secondhand shops and these are equally unpretentious and serviceable. Just as effective are the type of tables often seen in cafés or French brasseries. Bentwood tables, tables with wooden tops and cast-iron legs and even more modern designs with glass set in a plain metal framework all fit into the country idiom. Marble-topped bistro tables double up as excellent surfaces for rolling out pastry.

Extend the same spirit of improvisation to your choice of dining chairs. There is something deadening about the matched dining-room set. Chairs which have some kind of family resemblance but still differ from each other in some small detail inject an element of wit and individuality. You could collect traditional country chairs, such as Windsor chairs, ladderback chairs, chairs with rush seats, carvers and the like. Do ensure, however, that they are all about the same height, and that this corresponds comfortably to the height of the table. Other collections might comprise Lloyd Loom basket chairs, bentwood chairs, Victorian balloon back chairs or any other style that catches your fancy and complements the type of table you have chosen. Really disparate collections can be given the appearance of unity by painting or staining them all a colour, stencilling a pattern on the back

An exposed brick fireplace provides a natural focal point for an informal dining table, with its overhead storm lantern (far left). The lack of bright colour in the room is more than compensated for by the textural variety: wood, brick and stone. A striped woven cotton rug defines an eating area (above). The ochre colour used for the built-in corner cupboard and extended to the dado rail is a traditional eighteenth-century colour.

rails, or upholstering seats in the same material. Long wooden settles, country benches or even reclaimed church pews, provided they are fitted with seat cushions, can also make good country-style seating.

Good lighting is another key factor in promoting comfort and relaxation. Even if the decoration of the room and the way the window is dressed make the most of available natural light, there will always be grey winter days when some supplementary illumination is needed. And at night, the whole character of a room can depend on the quality of the lighting. Bright, even, overhead illumination strips a room of character and interest. The table is best lit by

some form of hanging light, either a traditional pendant or a rise-and-fall design. Utilitarian metal shades, antique glass globes or beaded pendants, and the plainer styles of chandelier or branched fitting are all perfectly acceptable. A plain metal candelabrum will give soft, unbeatably atmospheric light. Wall sconces, either electrically or candle-powered, are a common feature of dining rooms: any side lighting, including small table lamps on sideboards or candlesticks, means that the main light does not have to be too bright.

Keep the rest of the dining-room furniture simple, functional and out of the way. There should be enough room all around the table for chairs to slide in and out easily; cramping a small room with heavy sideboards and corner cupboards will quickly diminish whatever pleasure you have in spending time there. If there is enough space, there are plenty of types of storage furniture for housing table linen, cutlery, china and glasses, many of which can also function as a serving area. The sideboard is the classic dining-room piece; alternatives include plain oak or pine chests, chests of drawers,

Small touches of colour – such as the painted blue chairs – enliven an essentially neutral room with its tiled floor and stone-coloured wall (left).

Flowers, like the brilliant red poppies, are another good way of introducing colour. This dining area makes use of a vivid blue to draw together different parts (right). The glass panel in the door, dragged dado and radiator, window frame, plate rack and candlestick are all the same intense shade, a foil for the warm tones of the paisley oil cloth and pelmet.

and even small buffet tables with drawers. The traditional country dresser with its racks of open shelves over a base comprising drawers and cupboard space is usually big enough to accommodate all the equipment you will need. And the open shelves make an attractive place to arrange china.

Just as it should be under- rather than over-furnished, the dining-room does not need much in the way of incidental decorative objects. Apart from the food and the

table setting itself, let decoration come from objects which have some useful role to play. A collection of antique tureens, old tin packaging, pretty plates displayed on the wall, cheese and butter dishes and coloured or engraved glass, even if they are not in daily use, have a homely quality which is well in keeping. On the walls, you can hang a good mirror, framed maps, or a collection of animal prints. Natural themes, and anything connected with food and drink, also make good subjects for paintings and prints.

THE LUNCH TABLE

Lunch is a sociable meal. Not as private as breakfast, nor as ceremonial as dinner, it is an occasion where simple hearty dishes can be enjoyed by family and friends in an atmosphere of warmth and informality.

Few people want to eat heavily in the middle of the day and it is no longer fashionable or particularly convenient for most

An exuberant combination of paint techniques: stencilling frames an alcove displaying superb trompe l'oeil *shelves; painted plaster fruit and vegetables make a three-dimensional picture above the mantelpiece (far left). Another kind of display is created by the sheer quantity of blue and white containers packing the shelves of an old pine dresser (left). The simplest lunch for one can still be a treat: fresh country bread, farmhouse cheese and fresh fruit could not be easier or more delicious (right).*

households to have the main meal at this time. But even if you don't plan to serve three elaborate courses, it still needn't be sandwiches: food should be appetizing, colourful and satisfying. Great simple lunches can be organized around one basic dish with an accompaniment of soup, salad, fresh bread or cheese. Pasta of various descriptions – from rich lasagne to penne with ham, cream and mushrooms or spaghetti with pesto sauce – make warming family lunches. Flans and quiches are also good standbys and can be made in advance. French onion tart, or *pissaladière,* makes an exciting variation to the standard egg and bacon pie; in the winter, there's nothing more satisfying than a traditional fish pie, full of scallops, prawns and mussels. When the weather is hot, the main dish can be a wonderful *salade niçoise,* grilled sardines, *moules marinières* or a bowlful of prawns to dip in homemade mayonnaise. Soups can be

a meal in themselves. Homemade tomato soup, fresh vegetable, onion or creamy vichyssoise, served with granary bread and some farmhouse cheese add up to a lunch of appealing simplicity.

When there are guests around the table, you may want to adopt a different strategy, and instead of serving one main dish, follow the tradition of Greek *meze* or American brunch and lay on a buffet of many small dishes. Stuffed vine leaves, stuffed tomatoes, grilled sausages or devilled kidneys, taramosalata and tsatziki give a Greek flavour; salamis, artichokes in vinaigrette, tuna and beans, and Parma ham and melon make it Italian: it can be helpful to think of dishes from the same part of the world when planning a luncheon party.

The type of presentation should come naturally from the food being served and the occasion. And you don't need an expensive dinner service to have style. Collect different

MAKE FROSTED FLOWERS TO DECORATE DRINKS OR DESSERTS: DIP PETALS OR SMALL FLOWER HEADS IN WHISKED EGG WHITE THEN IN CASTER SUGAR. LEAVE THEM TO DRY ON GREASEPROOF PAPER IN A WARM PLACE.

plates and serving dishes the way you collect dining-room chairs – a selection of dishes that have some common theme, be it period, pattern or colour, but are not precisely matched, have a ready charm. American Fiestaware is a range of crockery based on the appeal of such variety, with each service consisting of different vibrant colours that can be mismatched at will. In a similar fashion you could hunt out retro patterns in junk shops and market stalls – the checked and spotted designs of the Fifties, orange, yellow and green geometrics from the Thirties, or just old plates with a common pattern of flowers or fruit. A table set with subtly mismatching crockery has a natural gaiety and sense of fun.

At lunchtime there's no need to go in for fine napery. If you need to cover the table, plain oil cloth does just as well. Checked cotton or tablecloths in the strong shades of mustard, indigo or sage green also look good. A well-loved white damask cloth spread over a table set up outside in the sun always looks enchanting.

For a special summer lunch, make a petal ice bowl in which ice cream and fruit can be served. Place ice cubes in the base of a freezerproof bowl then place another smaller bowl on top and weight it down. Scatter flower heads and petals in the gap and fill with iced water. Freeze until solid. Remove from the freezer, gently detach the inner bowl and turn out the ice mould.

When the table is not in use, between mealtimes, bowls of fruit, nuts and decorative plates prevent the dining-room from looking unlived-in (above right). Branches of blackberries make an unconventional, edible display. Plates and other ceramics decorated with food motifs have a natural appeal in an eating room (below right). An old family portrait makes an unusual if benevolent addition to a country kitchen (far right). The figures preside over an eclectic collection of blue and white pottery, which is attractively displayed whilst being ready for use.

Informal flower arrangements, just picked from the garden, capture the right mood. But even if your flowers come from the florist, keep them seasonal. Potted snowdrops in a rustic basket make a delicate spring centrepiece; rose heads floating in a glass bowl look summery and romantic; or you can trail ivy, bright leaves or vines the length of a table for an impromptu autumnal effect. Be careful when displaying bright winter berries in your arrangements. Children can be very tempted to sample them, so be sure you know which ones are poisonous and keep them well out of reach.

Martha Stewart's Federal Farmhouse

At the top of a hill, looking out over Long Island Sound, is Martha Stewart's Connecticut farmhouse. Built in 1805, the house is typical of its place and time, with two chimneys, a central hall and four rooms on each of the two floors. Although the rooms are not very large, they are comfortable and airy, with good proportions and high ceilings. For Martha, a prolific writer on all aspects of entertaining, the main attraction remains the garden, despite the obvious appeal of the house.

Over the last 18 years she has been putting her gardening ideas into practice and learning as she goes along, taking as inspiration Monet's garden at Giverny as well as English gardens such as Upton House and Hidcote. In this south-facing farmhouse garden, there are many different roses growing on trellises, perennials and a pergola with clematis trained over the top. But, since Martha also gardens to eat, flowers share the space with many varieties of fruit and vegetables, mostly grown from seed. Tomatoes, peppers, aubergines, asparagus, soft fruit and fruit trees flourish here, protected from the wind by a stone wall and large perimeter trees.

Inside, in sympathy with its character and architectural detail, the house is furnished largely with

pieces from the early part of the nineteenth century. There are two kitchens. One is more of a studio, where Martha devises and tests her recipes, and is equipped with a variety of catering-sized appliances. The other, which is a kitchen for living as much as cooking, contains Martha's prized Aga, equally treasured by her five cats and two Chow dogs. With its hearth, iron stove and collection of old kitchen utensils, it makes a natural place for entertaining in the winter months.

In the summer, Martha likes to eat outdoors as much as possible, with meals planned around the bounty of the garden. A table might be set up in the dappled shade of the pergola and guests served all manner of fresh vegetables, fruit and salad, with perhaps a *frittata* (Martha also keeps hens) and berry tarts for dessert. She relies on herbs for seasoning, rather than spices, and naturally grows her own.

Her approach to the presentation of food is equally direct and informal. Unlike her furniture, most of the dishes, glassware and cutlery that she has collected over the years date from the latter half of the nineteenth century and the first part of this century. A delightfully mismatched and eclectic selection includes old Italian plates in turquoise and gold, delicately carved French bakelite flatware and dishes decorated with flowers and fruit. When Martha sets the table, she tries to choose dishes – such as majolica asparagus plates for asparagus – to coordinate with the food that she serves and each drink will be in a different type of glass. Such a lively mixture of pattern and colour creates a highly individual country table, the perfect setting for enjoying fresh garden produce.

CHAPTER FIVE

A Room
Of One's Own

EVERYONE NEEDS A TIME AND A PLACE TO PURSUE THEIR OWN INTERESTS. OVER THE YEARS A GREAT MANY WOMEN HAVE FOUND THAT ALTHOUGH THE WHOLE HOUSE MIGHT BE THEIR ULTIMATE RESPONSIBILITY, THERE SIMPLY WAS NOT A CORNER OF IT WHICH WAS TRULY THEIR OWN SPACE. NOWADAYS, AS MORE AND MORE PEOPLE ARE BASED AT HOME, A ROOM OF ONE'S OWN HAS TAKEN ON A NEW MEANING. IT HAS BECOME A PLACE WHERE ONE MAY WORK AND ACTUALLY EARN A LIVING RUNNING A BUSINESS.

An attic room, with its beamed ceiling and panelled walls, makes a perfect retreat, a place for work or study away from the daily bustle of the rest of the household.

IN THE GENEROUS COUNTRY HOUSES OF THE past, where there were plenty of rooms devoted to specific functions, there were always places where you could close the door on the world. For the gentleman, such a retreat was usually known as the library or study, a masculine enclave filled with comfortable leather armchairs, lined with books and with a faint aroma of tobacco. The lady of the house had the morning-room, a bright and cosy apartment on the upper floor where she could concentrate on letter-writing, reading or sewing without being interrupted.

The roles and the attendant lifestyles may be a thing of the past. But for most of us, the need for private space is as great as ever. Whether you just want some peace and quiet, or the elbow room to expand a serious interest into a profit-making concern, it is important to turn some place within the home into a room of your own.

ASSESSING YOUR NEEDS

It may sound like an obvious point, but before you set to work to convert the attic, or stake a claim on the spare room, it is vitally important to work out exactly what you want the extra space for and what this entails. If you have a specific pursuit in mind, have you considered all of your requirements? For an activity such as photography, for example, you will need a sink and running water, a room which can be completely darkened and a safe place for storing toxic chemicals. If you want to set up a pottery workshop, you will also need a water supply, a floor which is easy to clean and special ventilation if you are installing a

kiln. If your activity involves heavy equipment, a studio in an attic or on an upper level may mean that the floor will need to be strengthened. If you intend to set up in business at home, you may need to install a separate telephone line or even have a separate entrance for clients.

On the other hand, if you are just looking for a corner to yourself, you should still think about how it could best be organized. Do you need a place where you can leave papers, fabric or artist's materials laid out, for example, or are you prepared to pack everything up at the end of each day? Do you need privacy and quiet, or, in the case of a music studio, is there a chance that your activities might disturb others in the house? Think about whether you need natural light; if you are an artist, do you need north-facing light? Will you need special equipment, extra storage space or more power points? And do you need to remain within hearing distance of the rest of the household?

Answering these questions and making a list of all the elements you think you might need will help you proceed to the next step, which is finding the right space for your particular purposes.

ROOMS WITHIN ROOMS

For many of us, finding a 'room' of our own is just as much a question of attitude as space planning. If you don't need to shut yourself off from the rest of the house or intend to

A sunny corner with plenty of natural light is a good place for a reading table and chair. Finding extra room for such quiet pursuits is a question of attitude as much as space planning.

Lining a wall with book shelves is not only a visually attractive option — it also provides very effective sound insulation. Covering the wall behind with cork or thick fabric will make the shelves even more effective in preventing sounds from the rest of the house from invading a tranquil space.

indulge in any activity which involves special equipment, you might not need a separate room at all, just a different approach to the space you do have. You could simply designate an area within another room as a permanent base for study or relaxation. Your corner could be in a bedroom, in a section of the living room or dining-room or even in the kitchen if it is big enough. Find an area which is slightly out of the way of the main activities – in an alcove, at one end of the room or in a corner – and mark it out as your territory by the way it is organized and furnished. Equip yourself with a good desk in a traditional design, a secretaire or even a lovely old table, and ensure there is a chair which will stay in place without being commandeered for other purposes. Surround yourself with pictures, objects, books or photographs which make the space your own.

THERE ARE NUMEROUS TRICKS YOU CAN USE TO MAKE A SMALL SPACE APPEAR ROOMIER: USE GLOSS PAINT TO REFLECT THE LIGHT; PAINT WALLS AND CEILINGS IN THE SAME LIGHT SHADE TO UNIFY THE SPACE; IF BULKY ITEMS OF FURNITURE CANNOT BE REMOVED, CAMOUFLAGE THEM BY PAINTING OR COVERING THEM IN THE SAME SHADE OF PAINT OR FABRIC AS THE WALLS, CEILING OR FLOOR.

A little writing desk, in a living room corner, is set out of the main conversation area (above left). The accompanying chair is covered in the same fabric as the rest of the seating to give visual unity. A traditional fall-front bureau with drawers below is a sympathetic choice of desk in a bedroom (below left). Here landing space has been put to good use by adding a table and chair to make a place for reading (right). Plenty of natural light is supplemented with a reading lamp; any area used for study or close work must be adequately lit.

There are various decorating strategies which can help to separate activities further and make your working area more distinct. In a bedroom which doubles as a place to work, a tailored style of bed cover and scatter cushions can help to promote an atmosphere of the dayroom and make it easier to ignore the fact that you are working in the room where you also go to sleep. Setting up a desk or table and chair in front of the window, so that you sit with your back to the room, also helps. Elsewhere you might like to give yourself a little extra privacy by screening your desk or table from the rest of the room. A free-standing book-case set at right-angles to the wall, a metal stand holding a collection of luxuriant house-plants or a Victorian fabric- or paper-covered folding screen are all very attractive and effective solutions.

There might also be odd corners around the home which you could turn into a place of your own. Many older houses have considerable space under the stairs, which could be converted easily into a quiet corner for a desk and some shelves. If you add a table lamp and put a rug on the floor, you can create a comfortable feeling of enclosure. A large hall or wide landing might offer a similar opportunity for setting up a study area. Box rooms or redundant pantries could also be put to good use. Then there is the question of 'spare' or 'guest' rooms. In many homes a bedroom is maintained year-round for the sole purpose of accommodating guests for a few days. You may well decide that the time has come when your need is greater than theirs and requisition it. Keeping a day bed or convertible sofa bed

will mean that you can still have visitors but will free the room for more intensive use.

If there simply isn't a spare room and your particular needs are such that they cannot easily be met within a main living area, you might be able to create some self-contained space by partitioning off a section of a larger room. This strategy will allow you, for example, to create a study without sacrificing an additional bedroom.

First of all, you need to establish that the original room is big enough to be subdivided

103

comfortably: there's no point in converting one habitable room into two poky little spaces that no one can use for any purpose. Secondly, the room should be properly proportioned and lit. A large, regularly shaped room with two or more windows, preferably a pair on the same wall, makes an ideal candidate for this type of conversion. Each new room will have the benefit of natural light if the dividing wall is positioned accordingly and the new rooms will then also look natural in terms of their shape and proportion.

Finally, the work should be executed and finished off so that it is in keeping with the architectural character of the original room. Extend skirting boards and mouldings throughout the new areas and match any plasterwork details.

A beautiful Gothic mirror defines a writing area within a kitchen, the perfect place for catching up with correspondence, or keeping track of household accounts (above left). Filled with vivid artefacts brought back from travels in the East, this studio room is itself a source of inspiration for a ceramicist, whose work is displayed in the centre of the room on an antique pedestal table (below left). An attic bedroom doubles as a workspace for a fabric designer (right). If you are going to work in a bedroom, it is often a good idea to dress the bed to give it a more tailored appearance during the day.

UNDER THE ROOF

Some of the most useful – and wasted – space in many houses is right under the roof. An attic conversion can be a good way of getting the extra space you need without spending too much time or money. Provided that there is sufficient potential floor area with reasonable headroom, or that headroom could be easily created with the addition of dormer windows, this type of conversion is fairly straightforward. There are even companies which specialize in supplying conversion 'kits' containing everything you need, from access stairs to flooring. At some stage, however, it may be necessary to obtain specialist advice to make sure that what you are planning to do to the attic will hold up structurally as well as satisfy any planning or building regulations.

Attic retreats make good sense for all sorts of reasons. The work involved is usually simple and not too expensive; extra room can be gained without affecting the rest of the house or altering its appearance too radically; the new space will be generally warmer and brighter than an equivalent area in a basement. An attic is naturally self-contained, so there is no problem of privacy, and soundproofing, if necessary, could be carried out very easily. An attic would only

THE UNUSUAL PROPORTIONS AND FEATURES OF AN ATTIC BEDROOM CAN EITHER BE MINIMIZED, BY PAINTING WALLS, CEILINGS AND WINDOWS IN THE SAME COLOUR, OR ACCENTUATED, BY PICKING OUT BEAMS, STRUCTURAL SUPPORTS AND WINDOW FRAMES IN SHARPLY CONTRASTING SHADES.

be a bad choice of workroom if the work in question involved heavy machinery. It is unlikely that you would be able to strengthen the floor joists in a loft sufficiently to take the extra load.

The two main issues involved in converting a loft or attic are access and lighting. For a room in regular use, a pull-down ladder or similar arrangement will quickly become highly irritating and possibly unsafe, so a more permanent solution will need to be investigated, perhaps with the help of an architect or designer. You may have to sacrifice a little floor area from another room to achieve this.

Big country attics with generous dormer windows pose no lighting or ventilation problems. In most cases, however, you will either need to install roof lights or build dormers into the roof. Attics can be warm places, as heat rises through the house to collect under the eaves, and some efficient system of ventilation is a must if the room is going to be habitable and pleasant to work in year-round. It is usually an easy job to extend other services, such as electricity and water, into a loft space.

When a hobby becomes a more serious pursuit, it is well worth looking at areas within the home, or even outside it, to gain the space you need. Naturalists or archaeologists, with bulky trays of specimens, charts and equipment of various descriptions, may find the answer in a warm, dry attic where the materials needed for their research can be safely stored and left undisturbed. An alternative would be to convert any outbuilding, such as a barn, shed or redundant garage.

MOVING OUT

For enterprises on a larger scale you may have to consider moving a work area outside the home and into an outbuilding, a shed, an old summerhouse or even into an extension which you have built specially to accommodate the overflow. Or you might just wish to make that important psychological break between home and work by leaving the house to reach your study via a separate outside entrance. Older homes in the country often come with a selection of outbuildings of various descriptions, many of which are ripe for conversion. Old barns, redundant garages or sheds can make good studios or workshops for painting, pottery, metal- or woodwork – any activities which may require machinery and generate more noise and mess than you would want indoors. Less elaborately, you may just need somewhere quiet to get away from it all. An old summerhouse at the bottom of the garden could well fit the bill. You could add some insulation, extra weatherproofing and lay on electricity or telephone services to make a year-round home from home.

THE PERSONAL TOUCH

Now that you have a room of your own, the next step is to furnish, decorate and equip it. If you intend to use the room as a creative studio of some kind, decoration will be dictated by all the practical needs the space has to meet. If, on the other hand, the room is a home office or study, you can afford to be a little more elaborate in your choice of colours and finishes.

Modern machines and technology, such as computers and fax, have meant that working

MAKE A FABRIC-COVERED FOLDING SCREEN TO CREATE A SPACE OF YOUR OWN. STRETCH FABRIC OF YOUR CHOICE TIGHTLY OVER FOUR HOLLOW-CORE DOORS OR PIECES OF THICK PLYWOOD APPROXIMATELY 1.8 M × 0.45 M (72 IN × 18 IN) AND 2.5 CM (1 IN) THICK. SECURE THE FABRIC WITH STUDS AROUND THE EDGES AND ATTACH HINGES TO LINK THE PANELS. IF CONTRASTING FABRICS ARE USED FOR FRONT AND BACK, THE SCREEN CAN BE REVERSED FOR A NEW LOOK.

To recreate the elegant effect of the traditional wood-panelled library, investigate the wide range of reproduction mouldings now available in fibreglass, polystyrene, plaster and wood. Accentuate the panelling by highlighting the mouldings or using a different paint effect, such as ragging, within the panels; alternatively, keep the effect more subtle with a unifying treatment.

from home is a viable proposition for a greater number of people than ever before. And many are finding that they can live further away from main business centres and still function efficiently. But setting up a full- or part-time base at home does not mean that you have to import office style. It seems a particular shame to go to the trouble of establishing a work room at home and then duplicate the sterile environment of most city offices. One of the joys of working at

A painted cupboard is transformed into a cabinet of curiosities, as old leather-bound volumes are combined with an antiquarian's collection (above). A room of one's own can be a place to display the results of a lifetime's collecting. Rich in antique textiles, painted pattern and oriental artefacts this mysterious retreat provides a means of enjoying the diversity of the collection (right).

home is to be able to spend the day in a more relaxed and humane atmosphere, closer to the countryside.

There isn't a great deal anyone can do to disguise office machines, but there is no reason why their design has to determine the style of the rest of the room. Rather than hide the computer or camouflage the fax, it is best to display them for what they are and get on with making the rest of the room as comfortable and personal as possible. Forget matt black metal and white laminate and create the room you really would like to work in: it won't impair the efficiency of your machines if your home office is warm and inviting, and it could have a beneficial effect on you.

Panelling has traditionally been associated with libraries and studies and it makes a good choice of wall finish. Simple tongue-and-groove boarding can be applied all around the room and painted to create a snug atmosphere, or proper custom-built panelling can be recreated using softwood of some description fitted into a framework of mouldings. Attics can look very effective treated in this way. Panelling also helps to insulate against heat loss as well as forming an effective soundproofing. Another advantage of panelling is that it can readily be combined with a system of shelving or storage cupboards, giving a room a snug, fitted-out look.

Busy patterned wallpaper or striking paint finishes are usually inappropriate but there is no reason why you should not choose to paint the walls a positive colour or to hang curtains in a beautiful old chintz. For a fresh, morning-room atmosphere, choose light springtime shades of mint green, pale

primrose yellow or light rose to make the most of natural light. For warmer, richer colour schemes, choose dull golds, bronze, plum, or forest green for furnishing fabrics, complemented by cream, biscuit, or any other mellow off-white on the walls.

As far as furniture is concerned, pride of place should be given to the desk or table where you work. Although you may well need a specially adjustable surface for a keyboard or other equipment, a traditional desk or writing table will add immeasurably to the pleasure of having your own room. Good antique desks are investment purchases but there is a wide range of alternatives which can look just as handsome and cost a fraction of the price. There are many versions of the kneehole desk, with drawers at either side, most of which started life in commercial premises; rolltop desks with their array of pigeonholes and compartments; ladies' writing tables; even old kitchen tables can be pressed into service. Which type you choose will depend on the uses you have for it. Make sure you select a chair to go with the desk which is the right height and provides support for your back.

Good lighting is another essential. Arrange the furniture so that the place where you work has the benefit of natural light if at all possible. Several good table lamps positioned around the room, supplemented by an adjustable desk or 'task' light right next to the work surface, should be the basis of the artificial lighting. As always, dimmer switches will enable you to control the degree of light. For clear, even illumination of the work surface, it is hard to beat the classic anglepoise lamp.

STORAGE IS IMPORTANT TO KEEP PERSONAL PAPERS, MATERIALS AND EQUIPMENT SAFE. AS WELL AS THE CUSTOMARY SHELVES, CONSIDER OLD WOODEN FILING CABINETS OR PLAN CHESTS, FITTINGS SALVAGED FROM SHOP DISPLAYS, FREE-STANDING BOOKCASES AND, FOR EQUIPMENT YOU DO NOT NEED EVERY DAY, TRUNKS AND BLANKET BOXES.

A simple pine kneehole desk, with generous drawer space, is just as practical as modern office equipment and much more appealing (above left). Old wooden storage pieces, such as this set of drawers, are more at home in the country than their modern metal or plastic equivalents (below left). It is important to make a working space comfortable and attractive, a place you really want to be (above). A collection of favourite pictures and antique glass on the window sill help to induce a mood of calm and contemplation.

As far as the rest of the room is concerned, if you have the space to spare, an old leather armchair, a *chaise longue* or even a comfortable old sofa where you can flop at the end of a hard day will all go to create a working environment which is far removed from that of the clinical modern office. Don't forget to add plants and fresh flowers, pictures and even a few of your favourite decorative objects to ensure that your room is as welcoming as possible.

Tricia Guild's Morning Room

Tricia Guild, the creative spirit of Designers Guild, has achieved widespread recognition for her fabric and wallpaper designs, as well as her original approach to interior decorating. Tricia co-founded the company 20 years ago and has seen it become an influential and innovative force in the world of design.

For Tricia, an important part of her success rests on her ability to remain in touch with how the end product – her designs – will be used. Her ideas for designs arise directly out of her own preferences and experiences; in turn, the designs are then tried out at home. Tricia's house is not only a source of inspiration for her work, it is also where her ideas are often first put into practice.

For someone whose home is so intricately bound up with their work, a room of one's own is terribly important. Although Tricia lives in the heart of London, near the headquarters of Designers Guild, there is a distinct breath of country air about the place, a spirit of naturalness rather than a cultivated rusticity.

Tricia's own room – a 'morning' room in the truest sense, since the light is particularly good here at that time of the day – is the only new part of her house, an extension she commissioned when the house was first being renovated. Built on top of an existing ground-floor extension, the new room overlooks the garden, a vital aspect for Tricia, whose work is directly inspired by nature in its broadest sense and more particularly by flowers. The morning room has classic, contemporary lines and proportions and a light, airy feel. Directly accessible from the first-floor landing, there is nothing to block light from the skylight spilling down into the rest of the house. At the other end of the room, a balcony provides a vantage point from which to view the garden.

Although the rest of the house is intensely coloured and rich in detail, this is more of a calm and contemplative space, which refreshes the spirits and is ideal for creative daydreaming. Colours have been kept deliberately light and clear; pattern is restrained. A pale dusty pink covers the walls; upholstery is in plain blocks of pink, green and yellow, subtly balanced. The wooden floor has a painted pattern of green and white checks, creating a light, summery effect. Aside from the colours and the open views of trees and sky, the naturalness is reinforced by the texture of woven throws and simple rag rugs, important touches

of detail which give depth to the whole scheme.

One key aspect of all Tricia's rooms, evident here, is her use of flowers as a positive element of design, not, as in some cases, an afterthought or mere accessory. Flowers are not incidental in Tricia's rooms, nor in her day-to-day life. The changing displays reflect the seasons and what is happening outside in the garden;

the colours and form of arrangements add a vivid accent to the decoration of the room. Because she did not want this room to resemble a conservatory, all the flowers are cut, not growing. And while Tricia is an avid collector of pictures and ceramics, this room, unlike the rest of the house, has relatively little on display. The real pictures are what can be seen out of the windows.

CHAPTER SIX

THE COUNTRY KITCHEN

AT THE HEART OF EVERY COUNTRY HOME IS THE KITCHEN. THE SOURCE OF TANTALIZING AROMAS THAT PERVADE THE HOUSE — SOUP SIMMERING ON THE STOVE, BREAD BAKING IN THE OVEN, A CAKE COOLING ON A RACK — THE KITCHEN IS A SYMBOL OF WARMTH, FAMILY LIFE AND GENEROUS HOSPITALITY. THIS HAVEN IS A PLACE WHERE FAMILY MEMBERS COME TOGETHER TO DISCUSS THE EVENTS OF THE DAY OVER A CONVIVIAL MEAL OR WHERE GUESTS ARE ENTERTAINED INFORMALLY AROUND THE KITCHEN TABLE.

China dogs flank not a fireside, but a hob, in this warm and welcoming country kitchen. A sense of playfulness in the decoration keeps the atmosphere jolly and convivial.

IT HAS NOT ALWAYS BEEN LIKE THIS. DURING the nineteenth century, in the Victorian household, the kitchen was the domain of the cook, a formidable figure in most accounts of the time, who ruled her empire of scullery maids with a rod of iron. Then, rarely visited by the mistress of the house, the kitchen was as remote from daily life as it is possible to be, inconceivable as a living area. Even today, in some modern homes, the role of the kitchen as the centre of the household fares little better. Here the kitchen is equipped and furnished like a futuristic laboratory of food, with all the cold impersonality usually associated with a commercial catering establishment.

For most of us, happily, this notion is an alien one. The kitchen of our dreams is just as likely to be a place to relax with a pot of tea and a few friends as a place to try out a new recipe; it welcomes a school child with homework as warmly as a hungry horde ready for a meal. And the country kitchen is the place where your own modest harvest from the garden can be enjoyed to the full.

The unfitted kitchen

However haphazard and informal a country kitchen may appear, it still takes careful planning to organize an area so that it works efficiently. The country kitchen *looks* unplanned but is just as much the result of forethought and skilful adaptation as the most modern ergonometrically designed and streamlined version.

All kitchens should be based on the 'work triangle', which is nothing more elaborate than the routes between the sink, stove or oven, and the fridge. The aim of kitchen

COOKING RANGES BEGAN TO BE INTRODUCED AFTER THE ARRIVAL OF COAL IN THE EIGHTEENTH CENTURY AND REACHED A PEAK IN THE VICTORIAN AGE. MANY OF THESE ORIGINALS ARE STILL IN GOOD WORKING ORDER. TODAY'S CAST-IRON RANGES ALSO LOOK VERY COMPATIBLE AND CAN PERFORM A MULTITUDE OF USES BESIDES COOKING. HANG A SLATTED RACK FOR DRYING CLOTHES ABOVE THE RANGE, FOR EXAMPLE; WHEN IT IS NOT IN USE IT CAN BE USED FOR HANGING UP BUNCHES OF HERBS OR FLOWERS.

The stove is the true focal point of the country kitchen, serving as a place to dry clothes and warm toes as much as cook (left). Walls are painted a warm yellow, toning with the old tiled floor. An old country cupboard, with a rough painted finish and wire mesh doors holds crockery and glassware (above). Free-standing pieces such as this are every bit as accommodating and flexible in their application as fitted kitchen units, yet with much more individual character.

planning and layout of appliances is to ensure that these main routes are not obscured unnecessarily by any other traffic and that there is a logical progression from one activity to another. It is also a good idea to separate areas which get hot from fridges and freezers, if only from the point of view of energy efficiency. Once you have the main sequence worked out and are comfortable with the basic shape you can begin to add in the rest of the kitchen storage pieces and work surfaces.

Many country kitchens include an old-fashioned wood- or coal-burning stove such as the classic Aga, and the site of this main feature can be the starting point for your layout. If there is an existing hearth or open fireplace there may be enough room for the Aga to be installed in the space provided. Kitchens with adjoining sculleries, pantries or laundry rooms can lose most of the incidental appliances, freeing space for counters, dressers and tables. Freezers, dishwashers, washing machines and dryers could all be installed out of the way next door. A scullery would also be the place to install a deep butler's sink for washing large pots and pans.

If you do need to incorporate all the main appliances within the kitchen itself it is better to accept their modern aesthetic for what it is rather than go to elaborate lengths to disguise or conceal it. 'Country' finishes are rarely successful – plain white enamel is discreet and goes with everything. Stainless steel can also be surprisingly compatible with the country look. Occasionally appliances are hidden behind 'decor' panels which can be decorated in any fashion to blend in with other kitchen surfaces and finishes. If you really can't stand the sight of the fridge or washing machine, this is the best option.

Country kitchens tend to be less 'fitted' than the popular kitchens enthusiastically marketed by furnishing outlets. A slightly haphazard, old-fashioned look is a large part of their charm; the uniformity imposed by even the best fitted-kitchen style is somehow at odds with the country approach. By all

A larder is an indispensable part of the country kitchen (left). With outside walls and a stone or brick floor to keep the air temperature as cool as possible, the larder is a natural means of refrigeration. Here a rack for hanging game is now used as a pan rack. As appetizing as any grocery shop, with shelves of tempting provisions, this little glass-fronted cupboard stores spices, pickles and condiments out of the way but still in view (above).

Terracotta tiles inset with blue and white patterned tiles make a feature of the working area of this kitchen with its beamed ceiling and rough plastered walls (left). Blue and white is the classic kitchen colour combination; here, old china plates, the window frame, tiling and cupboard curtaining are all variations on the same fresh colour theme (below). This simple planked wall cupboard has been given a thin coat of grey, unevenly applied to show brush marks, and decorated with a simple stencil design (right).

means include a row of built-in cupboards under a wide counter or worktop, but rather than fill the rest of the kitchen wall space with similar units, opt for free-standing pieces such as the traditional kitchen dresser or cupboard for storing crockery, cutlery and glassware. If you have the opportunity to add on to the kitchen or make use of an adjoining room, you might consider installing a walk-in larder, with outside walls to keep the air temperature low. This form of natural refrigeration not only makes an excellent place for storing canned goods and preserves, it can also be used as a place for keeping cured meat and root vegetables.

A dresser holds a surprising amount of kitchen equipment and clutter, as well as providing a display space for all the pretty china plates, cups, jugs and tureens that you like to keep on show. Other free-standing pieces might include a butcher's block table for chopping and preparing food, or an old chest of drawers for storing table linen, place mats and cutlery.

SURFACES AND FINISHES

Practicality should be to the fore in any kitchen. Surfaces must be tough and washable, resistant to the effects of steam and heat, and easy to keep clean. Finishes should not be precious or highly decorated, but able to withstand daily wear and tear.

All of these requirements mean that kitchen decoration tends to be robust rather than subtle, hard rather than soft. Walls can be painted, sealed, panelled or tiled – but generally not papered. Blinds are often better than full-length curtains; floors should be durable and simple to maintain. At the same time, the kitchen will be an enjoyable place to be only if there is some attempt to create an atmosphere of warmth and welcome. Too many hard, clinical surfaces make a forbidding and cold environment, hardly conducive to promoting the joy of cooking – and eating.

The answer, to a large extent, is to use colour and small touches of pattern to dispel any hint of the food laboratory. Natural materials, chosen in preference over artificial ones, can also add inherent textural variety and interest which give a scheme a certain vitality. Colour is an important element to get right. Dark, vibrant colours are not sympathetic in a kitchen and will show up marks and knocks as well as creating a rather gloomy atmosphere in a room which is used as much during the day as at night. On the other hand, pastels somehow lack conviction in a kitchen and are not positive enough for creating the cheerful ambience that is so desirable. A better bet are strong, warm shades such as terracotta, yellows and creams, clear light blues and fresh soft

greens: which you choose will depend on the quality and degree of natural light the kitchen receives. Lighter, fresher shades suit rooms which get a lot of daylight; stronger, warmer colours counteract the effect of dullness in a room which is poorly lit.

And don't forget white. Brick or rough plaster painted with coat upon coat of pure chalky white makes an admirable kitchen finish. Perhaps because of the age-old belief that blue actually repels flies, blue or a bluish tinge has come to be associated with hygiene and cleanliness. White paint is available without the blue tint commonly added to

promote this 'brilliance' and traditional association with hygiene and gives a more subtle effect, ageing gently over the years without becoming at all dingy. Instead of painting plastered walls or brick you could simply seal them with a proprietary sealer. Natural or raw plaster has a dull pinky colour and a look of softness which makes it a good choice for a country kitchen.

Tiles create a practical surface, especially running along behind a sink, counter or hob where they provide a wipable splashback. Tiling also offers the opportunity to inject a little understated patterning which can give a certain edge and definition to the kitchen decoration. Simple checkered borders in blue and white, black and white, green and pink or blue and yellow, combined with plain tiles, make a crisp accent that can enliven an otherwise plain scheme. You can also inset special handmade tiles, perhaps displaying pictorial themes, in a plain tiled area.

ANTIQUE UTENSILS ARE VERY COLLECTIBLE ITEMS AND MAKE ATTRACTIVE KITCHEN DISPLAYS. START A COLLECTION OF OLD WOODEN BUTTER STAMPS, FOR EXAMPLE: THESE WERE USED TO PRESS DISTINCTIVE PATTERNS ONTO BUTTER ROUNDS AND EACH DAIRY HAD ITS OWN INDIVIDUAL MARK, OFTEN REFLECTING ITS GEOGRAPHICAL LOCATION.

Plain white walls are a natural choice for this kitchen with its wealth of natural surfaces and finishes: brick, wood and gleaming metal (below left). Old carpet beaters make an interesting pattern on the wall; Victorian coloured illustrations and prints of livestock pursue the country theme. Delightfully simple and appealing, this kitchen is organized horizontally with one long shelf, a rail for hanging things and a countertop running the full length of the wall (above right). Striped fabric conceals useful cupboards. An enamelled stove set into the wall has been emphasized by painting the recess a soft turquoise, adding a pine mantel over the top and displaying a cheerful collection of china cups, old toys and other homely items (below right).

Although real panelling is highly impractical in a kitchen, tongue-and-groove boarding, even to half height, can be both suitable and highly effective for walls which are not fitted out with storage units. This type of plain boarding looks especially good painted, Scandinavian-style.

And for a special decorative touch, simple stencilled motifs can look charming. Stencils do not have to be based on flower or leaf shapes, although these do of course blend in well with the country style. You might also like to try simple classical key borders or more geometric designs for a less feminine look, or opt for something more whimsical and amusing, such as the stylized chickens, fish or birds seen on spongeware crockery.

The other main surface area to consider is the floor. Carpeting, matting and even rugs are largely excluded from the range of options for reasons of practicality. Wood,

ceramic and quarry tiles, together with various forms of artificial flooring, form the basis of the kitchen flooring range. The classic country kitchen floor is probably quarry tiles: the mellow colour and natural appearance are strong advantages. Quarries come in dull earth shades of terracotta, black, browns and dull reds and can easily be laid in geometric patterns or checkered designs. But they do make a surface which is cold, noisy and rather unforgiving. A similarly natural-looking flooring is provided by brick. Laid diagonally, in basketweave or herringbone style, brick also works well as a way of visually connecting a kitchen with an outside area such as a terrace. Other hard surfaces include stone and slate.

Wooden floors of various descriptions are not so noisy, as well as being warmer under-foot. There is also much less chance that everything which drops will break, as is the case with tiles or stone. Waxed and sanded boards, new hardwood flooring and wooden tiles are all possibilities.

Despite its rather utilitarian associations, linoleum can be very successful. Avoid types which aim to simulate a natural material and choose plain tiles or sheet linoleum in good solid colours. A black and white checked linoleum floor is stylish and exceptionally practical, being easy to clean and fairly warm. You can make patterns very easily by using contrasting colours.

Just as soft flooring is impractical in a kitchen, too much soft furnishing in the form of curtains or elaborate fabric blinds is also inadvisable. Any window which is near a sink needs to be covered simply with a blind which draws up out of the way of splashes. But even if a window is not near the main cooking area, full floor-length curtains can hold cooking smells and quickly become dirty and discoloured. Light cotton gingham curtains to sill length, unlined floral prints, lace panels or plain slub weaves are all attractive and easy to take down for washing. Roller or Roman blinds screen light efficiently and cane blinds in natural, white or green also have a country flavour.

But there is often no need to cover a kitchen window at all. A sunny sill lined with pots of geraniums or a selection of herbs in containers may be all that is required. Or you could fit a window recess with glass shelves to display a collection of coloured bottles, spice jars or little glass vases.

An original tiled floor is a feature well worth preserving (left). Common in Victorian and Edwardian kitchens and halls, such floors are as practical as they are beautiful. This kitchen contains many other original details, from the overhead pulley-operated drying racks to the splendid Gothic door. Baskets, old birdcages and kitchen implements jostle for space, hanging from the planked and beamed ceiling (above). The mellow floor of old quarry tiles is echoed in the soft grey-green of the paintwork.

KEEPING IT ALL ON VIEW

The kitchen is one place in the home where you can make a positive virtue out of the need to keep equipment and utensils readily to hand. Gleaming rows of copper-bottomed pans, racks of polished knives, strings of garlic hanging from a hook, a stack of gaily coloured cake tins are as appetizing as they are useful. The decorative potential of food and food equipment can be exploited to the full.

125

An overhead metal or wooden rack with butcher's hooks hanging from it can be used to suspend a collection of saucepans, sieves, colanders, slotted spoons, ladles and other kitchen utensils right where they will be needed. Wall-mounted wooden racks over the sink can be used to drain plates or store saucepan lids. Pots, pans and casseroles can be stacked on cast-iron or metal tiered stands positioned beside the oven or hob. Knives

remain in good condition if they are kept in a wooden block or a magnetic rack fixed to the wall by the main preparation area.

There are a whole range of traditional containers which strike the right note in the country kitchen: stone jars for wooden spoons, basketwork or wooden drawer dividers for kitchen cutlery, earthenware bread crocks or enamelled bins for loaves and rolls, tea caddies and painted metal tins for dry goods. Eggs gathered up in a wire basket, tomatoes ripening in a shallow green bowl, or a pile of lemons on a glossy black platter are also part of the country kitchen appeal.

Keep storage jars and spices on open shelves so you can locate the right ingredient quickly without having to fumble through a cupboard. Make sure there is enough room for your cookbooks, shopping lists and all the household clutter that always collects in a kitchen.

An antique panel forms the door to this china cupboard, packed with crockery, vases and glassware for the table (left). The simplest objects acquire a certain beauty when put on display, as these colanders show; a grey silk bow decorates a kitchen slate, useful for reminders and shopping lists (above right). Deep green tiles make a striking contrast to gleaming copper-bottomed pans and a collection of baskets (far right, above). The colours and textures of fresh fruit and vegetables are often enough to make an exciting kitchen display by themselves. Blue and white tiling and the display of basketwork containers strike a note of almost oriental simplicity (below right).

Bunches of dried flowers are the perfect way to decorate a kitchen year-round. Most varieties except hydrangeas can be dried simply by hanging them upside down in a warm place such as an airing cupboard. Remove the leaves, and hang in small bunches so that stems stay straight. The faster a flower dries, the deeper the colour.

Sir Terence Conran's Kitchen in Provence

Sir Terence Conran's kitchen in Provence is not a typical Provençal kitchen. These tend to be small and dark, as well as rather cluttered. Not one of these adjectives applies here, which is not surprising considering that the kitchen was designed by the creator of Habitat, who has spent his life promoting the beauty of simple, useful, everyday things.

Sir Terence, best known for his innovative approach to retailing, also has a passionate interest in food and cooking, an interest which has led to the creation of the highly successful London restaurants Bibendum in the Michelin Building and the Blueprint Café in the Design Museum. Here, in France, Sir Terence has created a kitchen which brings together his love of cooking and his fundamental beliefs about design,

yet which is flavoured by its setting amid the hills of Provence.

The kitchen, with adjoining laundry and larder, was converted from a barn when Sir Terence bought the nineteenth-century farmhouse several years ago. Two enormous French windows open onto a view of the farmyard and an avenue of chestnuts; the walls and beamed ceiling are painted white, with rafters in pale blue-grey; the new floor is stone. With natural ventilation allowing air to flow through the room, it is cool and airy, a perfect summer kitchen.

The basic organization is equally simple and effective. One wall is devoted to the working part of the kitchen, with hobs, ovens and stoneware sinks inset along its length. There is a continuous oak work surface, above which runs a broad oak shelf which takes all pans and casseroles used every day. The wall area in between is tiled in rectangular cream 'metro' tiles.

In the middle of the floor a huge oak work table divides the working area of the kitchen from the eating area. With drawers for cutlery and gadgets and a knife rack at one end, the table is big enough for three people to work comfortably side by side. Made in Sir Terence's English workshop, it is constructed of rough oak planks, full of knots and character.

The other side of the kitchen,

the eating area, is dominated by a wall of display shelves, which hold all the plates, dishes, bowls and mugs in daily use. Many of these – earthenware or porcelain, cheap or precious – are from the region. At waist height is a white marble cantilevered shelf.

Above the marble shelf, an angled strip of mirror reflects a feast for the eyes – bowls and platters filled with colourful locally grown vegetables and fruit.

And parallel to this wonderful display of fresh produce is an oak dining table by Ed Nicholson, more refined in detail and workmanship than the work table.

Provençal herbs grown on the rocky hillsides scent the air and flavour the food. Local markets provide the ingredients which delight the eye as well as the palate. This kitchen, with its sense of clarity and light, is a celebration of the true beauty of Provence.

KITCHEN COMFORTS

What finally transforms a kitchen from a work area to the centre of the household may have little to do with cooking. Providing a degree of comfort will encourage guests to linger and keep the cook company. There's no reason why a kitchen shouldn't include a sofa if there's enough room, or at least a comfortable armchair. An antique settle or a rocking chair would offer a similar sense of welcome.

Lighting has a great deal to do with getting the atmosphere right. In the kitchen there is a need for fairly bright directional lighting to illuminate work areas safely and efficiently. But this does not rule out the possibility of more subtle effects. Angled spotlights or downlights over the main cooking area can be combined with dimmable pendants over an eating area or table lamps in an alcove. The simplicity of glass globes or plain metal shades is infinitely better than self-conscious reproduction styles.

Most of what is displayed in the kitchen will be functional. But there is always room for little decorative touches. Food is a good theme for pictures and objects. A collection of prints of herbs, vegetables or animals, posters showing fish or seafood, antique signboards or packaging all give a kitchen character and a sense of fun.

A COUNTRY HARVEST

Much of what goes on in the kitchen will be in the nature of daily routine, getting meals and clearing them up. But the kitchen can also be the place where you exercise your creativity and imagination, making use of all the good things from the garden.

Bunches of herbs and flowers hanging from a length of rough twine festoon a kitchen hearth (above). In the country, kitchen decoration grows naturally from the activities of cooking, preserving and preparing food. Preserving, pickling and bottling are all ways of enjoying the harvest from your garden year-round. Recipes may be passed on from generation to generation; or you can experiment to find your own favourite combination of flavours (right, above and below).

In any garden there will be times of abundance and times when very little is available. Many of the traditional cooking and preserving skills are ways of husbanding resources so that produce can be enjoyed year-round, even when the garden is in its fallow period. Fresh vegetables, picked right from the garden, need little preparation or embellishment. Few of us taste really fresh food and that experience alone is worth the effort of growing a vegetable plot. But there is the question of what to do with all the food you can't eat. Pickling and preserving are ways of capturing the summer goodness and keeping it to enjoy later in the year.

Fruit can be stewed, turned into jam and preserves, or bottled whole with spices and brandy or kirsch. Fruit purée, such as apple sauce, can be frozen, as can whole strawberries and raspberries. Tomatoes are extremely versatile and can form the basis of many different types of ketchups, pickles and sauces. There are many excellent recipes for pickling and preserving fruit and vegetables; in time you will discover the confidence to make your own variations of flavour. And there is the added bonus that preserved or pickled foods make excellent personal gifts, particularly as Christmas or birthday treats.

Fresh herbs add zest to any dish. But since some herbs are annuals, they cannot be savoured in this condition all through the year. Herbs are easy to dry, however, and also look attractive displayed hanging in bunches or woven into wreaths or garlands. In the same way, it is always a good idea to grow flowers which are particularly suitable for drying to supplement fresh arrangements in the cold months of the year.

GOOD QUALITY OILS AND VINEGARS INFUSED WITH HOME-GROWN HERBS MAKE ATTRACTIVE GIFTS. USE OLIVE OIL OR WHITE WINE VINEGAR AND STRONG HERBS LIKE TARRAGON, BASIL, AND DILL. CRUSH THE HERB CUTTINGS SLIGHTLY AND ADD WITH THE OIL OR VINEGAR TO A CLEAR BOTTLE. LEAVE FOR 10–14 DAYS THEN USE AS A DRESSING OR MARINADE, IN MAYONNAISE, OR AS A FLAVOURING FOR GRILLED FOOD.

Barbara Kafka's Vermont Kitchen

The family home of cookery writer Barbara Kafka is the kind of white clapboard farmhouse that is traditional in New England. It dates back to the end of the eighteenth century when Vermont was first settled. A new kitchen was built when the house was extended and this large, comfortable room is now the centre of Barbara's culinary activities.

With its cast-iron stove, Shaker-style table and wooden kitchen cabinets, the kitchen has a relaxed country atmosphere and an appealing lack of pretension. The trestle table, a Shaker design, and its accompanying rush-seated chairs were actually home-assembled from a kit by Barbara's husband and daughter. Typically Shaker is a detail on the back leg of each chair. A peg allows the chair to be tilted backwards without being weakened: a feature which reveals what Barbara calls the 'Shaker sense of functional luxury'.

Barbara cheerfully admits to being an 'amasser'. A pie safe, jelly cupboard and sideboard provide her with the opportunity to display part of her collection of ceramics. This includes old blue and white pieces, spongeware, contemporary stoneware by Vermont potter Malcolm Wright, turquoise and opaline pots, ironstone which she enjoys for its wonderfully Baroque shapes, as well as decanters and locally produced wooden plates of thin turned birch burl.

Unusually, for a writer who is best known for her exploration of the potential of the microwave, Barbara also finds a use for much earlier forms of technology. The cast-iron stove, found in the house when Barbara moved in, is no redundant decorative feature. In the winter, stoked with wood, it provides an excellent way of

garden. Barbara is also an 'amasser' when it comes to planting: not one, but half a dozen different varieties of any given herb fill the herb garden, while in the vegetable patch are most of the vegetables that can flourish in Vermont's climate of sharp winters and intense summers. The conditions favour fruit-growing and there are many old varieties of currants, raspberries and blackberries. Summer is a time of intense activity in the kitchen, when anything which cannot be eaten there and then is put up for future use in some form or another – vinegars, pickles, jellies, sauces to be kept in the freezer and preserves of every description ensure that nothing is ever wasted. Barbara has also discovered that if you dry herbs in the microwave, they keep their colour better.

The working part of the kitchen is a sympathetic blend of modern technology and traditional fittings. There are three microwaves, but also an old butcher's block and a batterie de cuisine suspended from grappling hooks. There is a modern hob – dropped low to suit Barbara's height – but also an old pine table. Whether it is a question of drying herbs in a microwave or stir frying on a vintage stove, old and new are effortlessly combined in this productive New England kitchen.

cooking roasts, such as duck. Barbara also uses the stove for stir frying; by taking out the rings she can set a wok right down into the heat. In the summer, when it is too hot to have the stove blazing away,

it becomes a place to store and display the produce from the garden, heaped into baskets and old earthenware dishes.

The large windows draw in the landscape of fields, hills and

133

CHAPTER SEVEN

BATHROOMS TO LINGER IN

BATHROOMS ARE ALL ABOUT MOOD. THE WELCOME FEELING OF PEACE THAT FLOODS OVER YOU AS YOU CLOSE THE DOOR ON THE REST OF THE HOUSEHOLD AND LUXURIATE IN THE TUB; THE SENSE OF DEEP RELAXATION AS YOU INDULGE YOUR SENSES TO THE FULL; THE REFRESHING LIFT TO YOUR SPIRITS AS YOU SOAK AWAY STRESSES AND CARES IN WARM SCENTED WATER. ALL THIS DOES NOT ARISE BY ACCIDENT – IT TAKES PLANNING, DECORATIVE FLAIR AND A DEGREE OF IMAGINATION TO CREATE AN ENVIRONMENT THAT IS CONDUCIVE TO SUCH A MOOD.

Rough planked walls and an unusual wood-rimmed bathtub show that bathrooms can be delightfully quirky.

YET IT IS NOT UNCOMMON FOR THE BATHROOM to be relatively neglected in terms of decoration, which is all the more surprising when we consider the many needs it must serve. In some houses the bathroom has all the appearance of an afterthought. A jumble of fittings crammed in a small awkwardly planned space; a bare clinical cell which is far from enticing; a severely functional room where all sense of comfort has been banished – these are not untypical examples. In older properties bathrooms have often been installed in rooms originally intended for another purpose. But even in more modern homes the opportunity has often been missed to create a room where you really want to spend some time.

Many of the elements that go to make a successful bathroom could not be simpler. On one level, details such as a pile of thick snowy towels, a jug of fresh flowers or a tiled border around the tub can lift a bathroom out of the ordinary. At the same time, you must start with a good foundation: and that means above all the right fittings in the right place.

GOOD PLANNING

The problem with many bathrooms is that they are too small. When you consider that this is a room that everyone in the household is going to use several times a day, and that its overall atmosphere and efficiency will make a tremendous difference to the way you feel, it seems positively perverse to allocate it such a small area. If you have the option, it would be worth considering moving the bathroom into a larger room – a spare bedroom, for example – or dividing

a large room into a bathroom and a smaller bedroom. In terms of ease of planning and comfort, there is no substitute for space. A room-sized bathroom allows all sorts of possibilities for layout and furnishing which ultimately will benefit the whole household.

In a large bathroom, you can install the bathtub so that it projects out into the room at right angles to the wall, giving access on all sides. This type of arrangement makes bathing a positive experience and allows you to enjoy the decoration and furnishing of the room to a greater degree. In a large bathroom, there will also be space for double basins or a pair of basins, which can considerably ease pressure on the bathroom during peak periods. And there will also be the opportunity to site a lavatory or bidet well away from the bath.

If you have no choice at all in the matter and must put up with a small room, you

Brass taps and details, solid classic fittings and a simplicity of decoration add up to the traditional country bathroom. The draped window treatment – simply a length of snowy cotton wound loosely around a pole – and weeping fig soften what might otherwise have been too bland and plain a scheme. A vase of fresh flowers and a comfortable chair set an elegant tone. The bathroom, far from being a severe and functional place, should be a room where you positively enjoy spending time.

such as the roll-top claw-foot bathtub and the deep porcelain sink with brass fittings. The generous, classically designed tubs and sinks of the early decades of this century – the type of design one might associate with a good Thirties hotel – also strike the right note. A well-stocked architectural salvage yard might be able to supply original examples of these types of fittings; otherwise you might like to try companies which specialize in reproductions.

Naturally, modern bathroom fittings are another option, although generally they lack the character of the old designs. If you opt for a modern range, restrict your choice to the classic, simple styles in cast-iron or pressed steel and at all costs avoid coloured suites. White is usually the only colour worth having.

SURFACES AND FINISHES

As in the kitchen, the bathroom imposes special requirements for surfaces and finishes. The chief one of these is that all bathroom surfaces must be waterproof to a great degree, able to withstand both accidental splashing and the effects of constant steam or humidity. At the same time, walls and floors must be easy to keep clean.

This pretty bathroom, with its pink patterned paper and well-chosen accessories, has been decorated and furnished with as much attention as the most public room in the house (above left). Decoration can create a sense of tranquillity which is important in a room devoted to relaxation (right).

To make a herbal bath sachet, place a handful of fresh herbs in a square piece of muslin and gather the corners together to make a drawstring bag. Make a loop and suspend from the tap under running hot water.

have to work that much harder and exercise a little ingenuity to get the layout right. In a really small space, you may consider substituting a shower for a full-length bath or installing a sit-down or corner tub. Small-size basins are also available; those that project from the wall with no support underneath are good in a confined space. You might also think about having the toilet in a separate cubicle so that the bathroom can be devoted just to washing and bathing.

Choice of fittings is another important aspect of bathroom planning. In fact the style of fitting will go a long way to determining the overall style of the bathroom. Country bathrooms are always in some sense nostalgic places, with the emphasis on traditional comforts rather than modern functional design. In this context it is hard to beat old-fashioned Edwardian or Victorian fittings,

And floors must be safe, too. A surface which becomes very slippery when it is wet is dangerous.

Because of the constant contact with water or moisture it is a good idea to give particularly vulnerable areas extra protection. This can take the form of panelling with tongue-and-groove boarding or, more typically, tiling. Panelling is an attractive solution which can provide an important sense of unity. The panelling can be applied to the side of the tub and around the walls to half height; and it can enclose the basin or toilet cistern and plumbing in a way which combines concealment with the provision of

Pine panelling has been wittily painted with a freehand pattern of vines that wanders over the walls (above). The slatted blind echoes the cane chair; a splendidly proportioned bath is positioned under the window in the sun. Trompe stonework, on the walls and on the bath surround, creates a severe, almost ecclesiastical atmosphere in this bathroom (above right). Powder-blue tongue-and-groove panelling unifies the decoration, setting off a collection of nature prints and the family portraits (below right).

storage. Enclosing the bathroom in this way draws all the surfaces together, looks neat and finished and gives a certain sense of warmth. The panelling will need to be varnished to make it waterproof and often looks best painted in a clear light colour.

Tiling is a classic bathroom finish. It can be applied in panels around the bath or basin as a kind of splashback, or extended up to waist, shoulder or ceiling height. It usually looks neater if there is some visual reason for stopping the tiling – aligning it with a windowsill, for example, looks more considered than just stopping it at a more arbitrary point. Even using plain-coloured tiles you can vary the effect a great deal by your choice of tile size and shape and by the way they are laid. Tiny mosaic tiles produce a rhythmic gridded look, whereas rectangular or lozenge-shaped tiles have more of a Thirties appearance. Standard square tiles can be laid diagonally for more interest. And, as in the kitchen, large expanses of plain tiling can be effectively offset by coloured or checked borders to give a graphic quality. In a traditional bathroom, avoid jazzy patterned tiles and hot vibrant colours. Classic white, cream, pale pinks, greens and blues are more sympathetic. Neutral tiling is often the best choice, especially in a small room, but quite deep, strong colour can be used in small quantities as an accent or border. And you can always inset more expensive handmade tiles in a plain background.

The remainder of the wall area is usually best painted. Specially treated wallpapers are available for bathroom use and as long as their application is restricted to the upper portion of the wall they will not suffer undue

USE CERAMIC PAINT TO STENCIL ON TILED SURFACES IN THE BATHROOM – THIS WILL BE MORE PERMANENT THAN ACRYLIC PAINT OR STENCIL CRAYON. A FINAL LAYER OF VARNISH WILL GIVE ADDED PROTECTION.

damage. But painting is generally more practical and resilient and can be renewed more readily. Emulsion is generally not advisable in a bathroom; waterproof egg-shell is by far the best finish.

Bathroom colour schemes should be worked out with some sensitivity. This is a room where natural light is important; dark, dramatic effects are out of place. And because the bathroom is often quite small, it is not advisable to introduce too many colours or patterns. A basic neutral background colour enlivened with sharp accents of black, dark green or ultramarine can be very effective. Alternatively, choose a light, clear colour as a foundation and add a couple of near shades or tones to it. Watery colours, such as aqua, turquoise, and all the blue-greys are soothing and peaceful. The bleached, sandy palette of beiges, dull rose, creams, ivories and light golden brown go well with a bathroom which includes many natural textures and finishes. If the room receives a lot of warming sunlight, a pale green shade can be very refreshing.

A painted floral border gives distinction to a basin set in an alcove. The colours – sage green, ochre and dull red – have a nineteenth-century look which goes well with the style of the mahogany mirror (above right). A wall of useful storage is concealed behind discreet panelling. The antique tub is positioned at right angles to the wall, which gives a great feeling of space and comfort (below right). A marbled dado and sponged walls form the elegant background to a bathroom full of fine details and fittings (far right). The Gothic arched mirror behind the bath complements the architectural detail.

On the floor it is often best to avoid carpet, which can become rotten. Tiling in ceramic or linoleum tiles is highly practical: black and white checked tiling is a classic bathroom floor. Natural matting in seagrass or sisal has an appealing textural quality. Wooden floors should be well sealed to protect against moisture, but can look exceptionally pretty painted a light colour and stencilled with a border, geometric pattern or repeating motif. Because bathroom floors tend to be hard, easy to clean and moisture-proof, they are also often cold underfoot. Make sure there is a deep bathmat, soft rag rug or cotton dhurrie ready when you step out of the bath.

PLANTS WHICH THRIVE IN THE HUMID, SHADY CONDITIONS OF A BATHROOM INCLUDE: FERNS, THE SPIDER PLANT, ASPIDISTRA, GRAPE IVY, THE UMBRELLA PLANT *Dracaena marginata*, THE WEEPING FIG AND PHILODENDRONS.

The fresh mint green of this bathroom, top lit by a skylight, creates the atmosphere of a conservatory (left). The bathtub is set in a tiled alcove, on a platform screened by a large potted palm. A Moorish look has been created here with a coloured glass light and an old filigree mirror frame: a refreshing sanctuary in a hot climate (above). Natural colours and textures are combined for a supremely soft look. Lace over openweave cotton at the window filters natural light (above right).

You can alter the appearance of a bathroom to a great extent by the way the windows are treated. Changing the glass in a window is a relatively easy proposition and can make an enormous difference to the quality of light. Remove nasty pebbled glass or any modern ribbed or textured finishes and substitute either plain frosted or sandblasted glass or etched, engraved or coloured panes. All are effective at screening for privacy but provide unbeatable delicacy and charm. Judicious use of mirror can also multiply the effect of natural light, dissolve space in a small area and generally give a bathroom a sparkling lift. Too much mirror, however, can be demanding in terms of cleaning.

If the bathroom windows are fitted with semi-opaque glass, there is no real need for any further covering. If you do want curtains or blinds, the merest suggestion is all that's required. Great billowing lined drapery is out of the question. Simple sill-length cotton curtains in checked gingham, a jaunty nautical stripe or a fresh floral sprig are good solutions. Neat roller or Roman blinds work equally well. For a more romantic look, evocative of an earlier age, you might like to hang a panel of antique lace from a fine brass rod, or drape a wisp of filmy muslin over a painted wooden pole.

Baskets make good bathroom storage. Choose plain wicker or paint the basket inside and out to match the colour of the walls. Seal with a coat of varnish to protect the finish and line the basket with a fabric lining. Gingham or a small floral print would be a pretty choice; gather the top to make a good fit.

BATHROOM STORAGE

How much you are able to store in a bathroom will depend on how big it is, but you will need a combination of concealed storage for proprietary products you don't want on view and open shelves or ledges for bathroom accessories.

The luxury of a large bathroom means that you might consider keeping linen and towels right to hand in a painted wooden cupboard or armoire. In a smaller space, a wicker hamper would do for laundry or for keeping such items as extra toilet rolls, toothpaste and the like hidden from view. In most bathrooms you will need some kind of wall-mounted cupboard, preferably lockable, where you can keep medicines safely out of the reach of children. Modern medicine cabinets can be distinctly lacking in charm and character; adapt your own version by painting a Victorian pine cupboard in an interesting shade.

Glass shelves fitted on chrome brackets have a traditional look; painted or stained wooden shelving fixed to the wall is a more rustic alternative. Baskets are handy for

Wooden lockers, a panelled ceiling and bath,
and individual details such as a ship's clock on
the wall extend the nautical imagery usually
associated with a bathroom and create the cosy
effect of a ship's cabin (left). A cane dresser
provides plenty of space to store all the bathroom
paraphernalia and display antique scent bottles
(below). Crisp shades of Oxford blue and a vase
of fresh flowers make the most of a small
bathroom (above right). Stonework washed with
burnt ochre and a filigree mirror suggest a
Moorish setting (below right).

147

A collection of silver containers, used to keep scent, powder and bath oils, makes an elegant display (left). A feature is made of very rough walls in this grotto-like bathroom (below). A bird in a cage casts its 'shadow', a whimsical trompe l'œil on the wall opposite. Treasured prints and a collection of personal possessions, a table to house books and magazines and slightly worn, familiar furniture make this a room to spend time in (right).

FLORAL WATERS FOR THE BATH OR FOR USE AS SCENT CAN BE MADE WITH MANY FRESH FLOWER PETALS. IN A SCREW-TOP JAR COVER PETALS WITH BOILING WATER, ADD 2 TBSP ETHYL ALCOHOL TO 1L (1¾ PT) WATER AND REPLACE THE TOP. SOAK FOR 1 WEEK, SHAKING EVERY DAY, THEN STRAIN INTO GLASS BOTTLES.

keeping tidy children's bath toys, fresh face cloths and hand towels or a collection of toiletries. Wooden or metal bath racks can hold soap, bath sponges and loofahs.

DETAILS MAKE A DIFFERENCE

Bathrooms are fun to accessorize: details do make all the difference between a room which is bland and featureless and one which is buzzing with interest and wit. Although bathrooms are visited frequently, they are generally not occupied for long stretches of time, so you can get away with adopting a visual theme for the decoration, a strategy which might be tiring in a main living area.

The association with water means that nautical or marine imagery can be amusing and evocative. Shells in a glass container, prints of sailing ships or seaside scenes, striped cushions or curtains and a blue-grey colour scheme can deftly suggest a watery world. A period flavour is simple to create and particularly appropriate in a country setting. If there is enough room, include an antique washstand and jug or an old wooden

clothes horse for hand towels and linen. Hang needlework pictures on the wall, lace at the window and display a collection of pretty china soap dishes. A bathroom can celebrate the honest beauty of natural materials: matting on the floor, loofahs and sponges, a dish of bleached stones and subdued neutral colours would emphasize this theme. Or you could borrow elements of the conservatory and create a lush exotic retreat with a painted cane chair, moisture-loving plants, coloured glass bottles and shallow bowls of pot pourri.

The bathroom, with its humid atmosphere and warmth, can be a good place for plants if there is enough natural light (above). But even if the conditions are less favourable, there are many hardy varieties which will flourish almost anywhere. Greenery always looks fresh in a light, bright room; here, patterned pots complement the tiling. Directly adjacent to a terrace, this bathroom is simply finished and decorated so as not to detract from the great sense of connection with the outdoors (right). Plain white planked walls and a black and white tiled floor make a suitably plain and homely background.

Jane Packer's Pot Pourri

The sense of smell is one of the most vital of all of our senses. The power of certain scents to trigger memories, provoke associations and set off trains of thought is undeniable. Perfumes or scents can also create an atmosphere of relaxation or luxuriousness, particularly appropriate in a bathroom where the emphasis is on comfort.

Jane Packer, the celebrated floral designer who also runs her own school of flower design, believes that we have rather neglected the sense of smell. Many flowers which were once scented have lost this characteristic through years of specialization and breeding; as a substitute we surround ourselves with harsh synthetic smells which diminish our ability to distinguish between subtle flavours and scents. A case in point is pot pourri, which all too often has an overpowering smell quite unrelated to the natural scent of flowers.

Only a few flowers, such as lavender, keep their scent when dried. To make any pot pourri, it is therefore necessary to restore the smell artificially, either by adding oils, or by making a dry pot pourri with spices such as cloves, aniseed, cinnamon, and dried citrus peel. Jane's version of pot pourri differs

from the usual one in two ways. First, she uses whole flower heads – tulips, peonies, roses and carnations – which retain their colour better than individual petals and have more visual impact.

Secondly, she adds natural oils to give an opulent, warm scent. The result has a certain faded elegance which is only one step away from fresh flowers.

Many people might feel that it is unnecessary to have any flower arrangement in the bathroom, dried or fresh. But Jane believes that flowers are an important aspect of any room where you expect to spend time relaxing and it is worth giving them the same attention you would give to the choice of towels or soap. Obviously, the scale of the display will be limited by space, but in this context, a small low vase of flowers or a bowl of pot pourri will have great impact. You can even include pot pourri in a very steamy bathroom: keep it in a jar and remove the lid when you want to let the scent escape – and enjoy pampering your sense of smell.

151

CHAPTER EIGHT

ROOMS FOR RELAXING

TRADITIONALLY THE DRAWING ROOM IS THE PLACE WHERE COMFORT, BEAUTY AND HARMONY REIGN. IT IS THE 'BEST' ROOM, THE ROOM WHERE YOU ENTERTAIN FRIENDS, RELAX BY THE FIRESIDE IN THE EVENING, READ, CHAT OR LISTEN TO MUSIC. IN THESE SURROUNDINGS, DECORATED WITH A LIVELY MIXTURE OF PATTERN AND COLOUR AND FILLED WITH TREASURED POSSESSIONS, YOU FEEL MOST AT HOME. THE RELAXED SPIRIT OF COUNTRY STYLE IS PERFECTLY SUITED TO CREATING THIS COMFORTING AND EVER-APPEALING ENVIRONMENT.

The rich, glowing patterns of old kelims blend naturally and effortlessly, a harmony of tones, motifs and design.

153

ONCE, IN THE GRAND HOUSES OF THE PAST, whole sequences of reception rooms accommodated a host of activities from music-making to dancing. And not so long ago, many houses had a front room or parlour shrouded in dust sheets for much of the year and opened up for special occasions, while everyday living went on in the back parlour or sitting room. Nowadays, there simply isn't enough space in most houses for a multiplicity of living areas and the living room may have to cater for many different needs.

It is the country living room, with its ease, informality and sure sense of style, which represents the perfect match between the traditional elegance of the drawing room and the busy demands of modern life. Architectural detail gives a sense of continuity; natural finishes and materials express the country spirit.

CHARACTER AND CHARM

The architectural character of a room is immediately visible both in its basic proportions and in the fine modelling and detail of different surfaces. Period mouldings and decorative flourishes always convey a strong feeling of connection with the past. The drawing room is traditionally the place for such elegance and refinement, where not only the best pieces of furniture and the finest wall treatments are displayed but also intricate carving and elaborate plasterwork.

In the recent past, there was a curious lapse of taste and sensitivity and many period houses were stripped of a whole range of ornament and detail – original fireplaces, cornicing, panelled doors and even skirting boards were lost in the impatient scramble to give old buildings modern interiors. This type of architectural vandalism is unthinkable today and anyone fortunate enough to possess an interior with original details generally keeps them in place. But there is always the problem of decay and disrepair; and, increasingly, with the high prices that architectural salvage can command, there is the new danger of theft.

Architectural details, such as cornices, picture rails and chair rails, are important not only because they demonstrate the presence of the past but also because they are a means of breaking up the expanse of a wall and giving it interest. This modelling of the surface is part of our visual vocabulary, an almost instinctive pattern or way of organizing space. If your house lacks certain features for any reason it is well worth going to the trouble of reinstating them, either by searching out original examples in scrapyards or architectural salvage companies or by obtaining really good reproductions of classic designs. You may not want to make this effort for every room in the house, but the living room really does benefit from the distinction of detail.

The key to successful restoration of this nature is appropriateness. The period has to be right, but also the scale and context. Fine Georgian mouldings do not belong in a nineteenth-century farmhouse, for example; you cannot install an Adam-style fireplace in a

Old chintz, panelled walls, an oriental carpet and treasured antiques – all the elements of the traditional country drawing room. The light, fresh colours and muted patterns keep the overall effect fresh and unpretentious.

AN ALTERNATIVE TO FILLING AN UNUSED FIREPLACE WITH FRESH FLOWERS CAN BE FOUND IN THE FIREBOARD OR FIRESCREEN. FIREBOARDS WERE WOODEN PANELS MADE TO FIT THE OPENING EXACTLY AND WERE USUALLY DECORATED WITH WALLPAPER OR *TROMPE L'OEIL* PAINTING; FIRESCREENS, PLACED IN FRONT OF THE FIRE TO MITIGATE THE HEAT, WERE PARTICULARLY LOVED BY THE VICTORIANS AND MANY FINE TAPESTRY OR PAINTED EXAMPLES CAN STILL BE FOUND.

An antique side table provides the place to display a collection of blue and white porcelain (left). The colour and pattern are subtly picked up in the cushion fabric and in the light tint of the wickerwork chair. Colour is in the details: a jolly collection of twenties and thirties jugs brightens up a mantelpiece, while vivid cushions pick up on the same paintbox shades (below right).

PRINT ROOMS WERE THE HEIGHT OF FASHION IN THE EIGHTEENTH AND NINETEENTH CENTURIES AND LADIES OCCUPIED THEMSELVES BY PASTING ENGRAVINGS DIRECTLY ONTO THE WALLS. RECREATE THE LOOK BY STICKING PHOTOCOPIES OF PRINTS, CAREFULLY AGED WITH A WASH OF TEA, ONTO A WALL. 'FRAME' THEM WITH PAPER BORDERS AND SEAL WITH A LAYER OF CLEAR VARNISH.

country hearth. You may well have to engage in a little historical research to see exactly what kind of details a house of your period would have possessed. Or you could always ask to look round a similar property whose interiors are intact. Strict authenticity is not necessary, although some people go to extraordinary lengths in their desire to be historically accurate. In fact, too pedantic an approach can result in an interior which more closely resembles a museum set than a real living room. In general, it is best to keep it simple if you need to replace mouldings with modern reproductions.

In a country house of some age, you may have the reverse problem. Old houses sometimes accumulate layers of addition; false walls and ceilings, modern finishes and dummy fireplaces conceal the original details beneath. If this is the case, restoration is more a question of stripping away than adding. The charm of old brick or stone walls, beamed ceilings and flagged floors was not always appreciated by previous generations.

In an interior which is not particularly historical and has very little in the way of character, just the suggestion of detailing might be all that is needed. A strip of wooden moulding, ready profiled and available off-the-peg from a timber merchant, can be applied around the perimeter of the room at waist height to make an instant dado. Paint the upper part of the wall a light colour and paper the lower part in a toning stripe, for example, and you will have created a period flavour without being too specific. Similar effects can be achieved by using paper borders, stencilled designs or banding to simulate panelling.

Occasionally more extensive work may be needed to remedy the situation. An unfortunate partition wall might have to be taken down to restore the original proportions of a room, a modern metal frame window replaced with a sash or casement, or a blocked-up hearth excavated and unbricked. You might also consider replacing modern flush doors with period panelled versions.

PATTERN MIXING

In the eighteenth and nineteenth centuries, the drawing room was always the place where decoration was rich and colours intense. The rest of the house might be plain and serviceable, but the drawing room proclaimed the status and taste of its owners. Although this tradition has been somewhat tempered today by the need for the living room to act as a comfortable centre of family life, there is still more opportunity to go to town with pattern, colour and finish.

You can achieve a sense of richness by the intensity of the colours you use, the quality of finishes, or in the mixing of pattern. The living room can take stronger colours than the rest of the house: clear yellows, jade green, rose pink or cerulean blue, for example. Although decades of white or pastel walls have made us a little hesitant when it comes to colour, in previous centuries there were no such reservations. Vivid colours make a perfect foil for paintings and fine furniture in polished wood, immediately giving a room a strong character.

The drawing room is also the place for interesting paint finishes. If you are using strong colour, it is important to apply it in

such a way as to give the surface depth and luminosity, otherwise the effect might be flat and dull. The past few years have seen a virtual explosion of interest in various broken colour techniques, from sponging and ragrolling to stippling and scumbling. In many cases, the results have not been entirely successful. Any paint effect, if applied with more enthusiasm than skill, runs the risk of looking insistent and crude, which is the opposite of the result you want. It is always a good idea to work with shades that are close in tone, rather than striking contrasts. Keep the marks of the tool you use subtle and understated rather than bold and obvious. With this degree of restraint, the techniques can be very effective indeed at maintaining a liveliness and sense of movement which is nevertheless easy to live with.

Paint effects are really just one way of creating a pattern on the wall. Self-patterned papers are another. Stripes, damask prints and the like can introduce a similar rhythm and interest without making too strong a visual statement. These papers, with their strong historical flavour, work well with dado rails, either covering the upper portion of the wall or the lower, and complemented by a toning shade. Printed wallpapers fell out of fashion in the second half of the twentieth century but are now enjoying a modest revival. There are many excellent historical reproductions and designs which are sympathetic in a country room. Perhaps the finest wallpaper designer of all time was William Morris. Morris designs have never

Terracotta walls make a mellow background in a low-ceilinged room (left). The opposite approach is taken in a room brimming with pattern: a Provençal stripe is expertly combined with bolder patterns in the same colours (below).

gone out of production and still retain their freshness and immediacy. Based on natural forms and designed in soft, glowing colour combinations the flowing patterns envelop and enclose a room without ever becoming too claustrophobic.

Pattern on the wall immediately brings up the question of pattern mixing. Unless absolutely everything else in the room is to be plain, you will have to work out some way of combining patterns sympathetically. Like strong colour, pattern mixing is an area which tends to make people rather nervous. And, unhelpfully, there are no real rules to follow to make the process foolproof: to a large extent, success comes with practice and confidence. But, if there are no hard and fast rules, there are some useful guidelines to bear in mind. For patterns to combine sympathetically there must be some kind of

R ING THE CHANGES THROUGHOUT THE YEAR BY ALTERNATING CUSHION COVERS WITH THE SEASONS. PIECES OF KELIM OR ANTIQUE FABRIC IN RICH, DARK COLOURS ARE IN TUNE WITH THE WINTER MONTHS; BRIGHTER PATTERNS, SUCH AS THE GLORIOUS PROVENÇAL PAINTED COTTONS, ARE IDEAL FOR SUMMER.

family resemblance, either in terms of colour or motif or both. A collection of kelim rugs, for example, is naturally harmonious because of the inbuilt similarity of colour and design. Patterns often go well together if there is a difference in scale but not of theme: a large full-blown cabbage rose print will look good with a dainty rosebud design. And geometrics seem to go with everything: a floral chintz with a pale green check or

stripe is a classic country combination. To save money and heartache, try out your ideas on a small scale first. Arrange snippets of the fabric or papers you intend to use so you can see how they look together before you commit yourself to an expensive and possibly mistaken purchase. While you are doing this, you should also be aware of the proportion of a pattern: the impact of a large-scale pattern will be vastly different on a cushion as opposed to sofa upholstery, for example, and a tiny sprigged design will have a radically different effect made up into full-length curtains than as a cloth covering an occasional table.

COUNTRY TEXTURES AND FINISHES

A large part of our enjoyment of any room, but particularly one devoted to comfort and relaxation, comes through texture and the sense of touch. Textural variety is important because it prevents a scheme from being bland and uninteresting, but it also helps to suggest, in a country setting, a certain ruggedness and rusticity.

The way the floor is covered or the material it is made of make an important textural contribution. Carpeting is the standard modern flooring, especially in the living room. But wall-to-wall carpet, although undoubtedly warm, practical and soft underfoot, can also be just a little too uniform. As a refreshing variation, try a large area rug, leaving a margin of stained, painted or varnished wood around the perimeter of the room. In the summer months, the rug could be rolled up and put away to give the room a cooler, lighter feel. Coir, seagrass or other natural fibre matting is

Panelled walls and cupboard fronts have been dragged in a shade of blue-green, in a subtle version of a distressed finish (above). Panelling, particularly softwood panelling, was traditionally painted. Here, by contrast, pine panelling has been stripped and left exposed to create a warm toned background (right).

supremely countrified and makes an excellent surface on which to lay a selection of rugs. And there are some new flatweave carpets on the market, including designs in muted stripes, plaids and checks. Flatweave carpet also has a period association, harking back to the striped and checked flatweave designs of the early nineteenth century. Wooden floors of every description also work well in the country living room, being practical, homely and rich in colour and texture. Wide stained oak boards, fine parquet or sanded, waxed or sealed pine all look equally good.

Occasionally hard floors such as flagstones, brick or quarry tiles extend right through the ground floor of a country house. In a living room, this type of surface can prove a little chilly and uncomfortable. Soften the effect with old oriental rugs, kelims, handmade rag rugs, hooked rugs or dhurries laid in overlapping layers.

CHAIRS AND SOFAS CAN BE DRESSED UP INSTANTLY WITH THROWS, AN INFORMAL TREATMENT IN KEEPING WITH THE RELAXED COUNTRY SPIRIT. ANTIQUE QUILTS AND TARTAN RUGS, KELIMS, BRIGHTLY PATTERNED INDIAN COTTONS AND EVEN SHAWLS CAN ALL BE USED.

Textural interest can come from a variety of other surfaces. In this spirit, a stone chimney breast, for example, should be left as it is, not rendered or plastered to blend in with the walls. Similarly, exposed beams or brickwork have an innate farmhouse appeal. Wooden dados, matchboarded ceilings and panelling can be painted or varnished depending on the wood. In general, panelling made of softwood such as pine was always intended to be painted because the wood is not of sufficiently high quality to be exposed. The same applies to window shutters and cabinet fronts. Unfortunately the recent vogue for stripping pine has brought to light many such features which do not stand up to close scrutiny. On the

A rich blend of patterns and country textures: plaster-pink distempered walls contrast with rough old beams, stone inglenook and carved fireplace (left). A variety of textiles in soft roses and reds, draped over sofas and armchairs, provides pattern interest. Draping furniture is the quickest and cheapest way of transforming a room, and is perfectly in keeping with country-style informality. Pattern can come from a variety of sources: framed motifs wittily echo the colours and pattern created by book spines (above). Disparate items are drawn together by a similar tonal range: a needlepoint chair and old velvet upholstery blend easily with an antique screen and carpet (right).

other hand, real oak or hardwood panelling has a beautiful grain and ages well.

Fabric also has a vital contribution to make when it comes to supplying textural interest. Living rooms naturally offer more scope for soft furnishing and upholstery than other rooms. Unless there are really fine working shutters or a window design of outstanding architectural beauty, curtains are an essential part of the country look. Antique or secondhand shops can be a useful source of period textiles in mellow colours and distinctive patterns. Rich velvet or old damask curtains with deep fringing; glazed chintz trimmed with braiding or gimp; coarser linen mixtures with rough open weave are inherently more attractive than many modern furnishing fabrics.

In general, the simpler the style of curtaining the better. Gathered headings hanging from a wooden or brass pole are more in keeping than either theatrical swagged drapery or crisp modern pleating. Combine with plain muslin or lace undercurtains to give extra flexibility and light control. And in the summer, you can remove the main outer curtains and enjoy the summery effect of semi-transparent drapery.

Upholstery can be a source of the same textural variation. Combine needlework cushions with worn leather armchairs; loose cotton covers with soft woollen throws; silk paisley shawls with chaise longues covered in velvet or fine wool.

As fresh and bright as the view, a window seat is upholstered in a light chintz and dressed with soft cushions, making an inviting spot for reading or daydreaming.

ARRANGING THINGS

Each period has its own characteristic scheme of arrangement, which, as much as the style of decoration, creates a distinctive flavour. Although fashion and taste undoubtedly came into it, there were often strong practical reasons for certain furniture layouts. In the eighteenth century, for example, drawing rooms tended to be sparsely furnished with light movable pieces which could be quickly assembled for conversation groups, by the fire or by the window as need dictated. By Victorian times, when heating was more reliable and artificial lighting more consistent, room arrangements became more static, fixed around the focal point of the fireside or a large circular table.

Today, with central heating and electric light the practical aspects of room arrangement are no longer as important. We don't need to be close to the fire for warmth or near a window for light to sew by. Instead we may have to consider how to reconcile different activities which may be going on in the same area, as the living room evolves into more of a family centre.

Chairs and sofas can be grouped in natural conversation arrangements served by occasional tables and side lighting. A fireplace makes an instinctive focal point for a seating group, as does a bay window or alcove: but never a television! You can also define a distinct area within the room by the use of a rug. A sense of balance is important. Symmetrical arrangements always look right but even if your room layout is less formal you should try to offset a large piece of furniture with several smaller pieces to provide equal visual weight.

This type of basic patterning can be extended right through to all the objects and pictures in the room. The living room is a natural place for display. Mantelpieces, table tops, glass-fronted cabinets or open shelves can hold a variety of collections, from china dishes and plates to old boxes, curios and photographs. The secret of making a good decorative arrangement is to mass individual things for impact, rather than dot them

Pure white chair covers and white walls are comfortable rather than clinical in this country version of the monochrome look (above). The rich detail of an antique quilt and lace curtains provides visual interest (right). An embroidered screen gives a seating area a distinctly oriental feel (above right). The very rough walls of this country drawing room have inspired a similar treatment for the bookcase (overleaf).

around the room. Group by colour, theme or material and then inject an element of surprise by adding the unexpected. Such collections can be greatly enhanced by good lighting. Concealed downlighting in an alcove, a lamp creating a pool of light on a side table or, more emphatically, a discreet spotlight picking out a plantstand or family portrait will all add immensely to the effect.

Pictures can be arranged following the same principle. A collection of prints in the same medium, showing the same subject or with similar tonality have greater presence when hung as a group. Or you can adopt an idea much seen in the Biedermeier interiors of early nineteenth-century Europe and arrange prints in a horizontal row quite low down on the wall above a sofa.

Finally, it is hard to underestimate the positive advantages of fresh flower arrangements, changing in scale, colour and character with the seasons and acting as a constant reminder of the garden. Concentrate on creating a sense of freshness and abundance, allowing tendrils and trailing vines to spill over the sides of containers and filling vases with clusters of blooms grouped naturally as if they were still growing.

THE ROUGHNESS OF COUNTRY TEXTURES MEANS ALL KINDS OF APPARENTLY UNPROMISING MATERIALS CAN BE PRESSED INTO SERVICE. SCAFFOLDING PLANKS CAN BE USED FOR SHELVING OR TO CREATE A BOOKCASE; DRAGGING THE PLANKS WITH A THIN WASH OF PLASTER GIVES THEM A STRUCTURAL APPEARANCE.

168

Mary Gilliatt's Country Comfort

Those who find decorating a process fraught with difficult decisions should spare a thought for the interior designer. Professionals, with all necessary knowledge at their fingertips, should, we think, find it easy to make up their minds and achieve the results they want. It may be reassuring to find that, like the rest of the population, they too can be unsure of their choices, feel confined by working to a budget and even make the odd mistake.

Mary Gilliatt, prolific author of books on interior design and decoration, as well as an interior designer in her own right, found it harder to design a room for herself than for her clients. She encountered two of the main pitfalls for the designer – being aware of so many options that decisions were difficult, and having a tendency towards an *idée fixe* which did not work out in practice. But she also discovered

the great strength of the professional, which is having the confidence to see the job through. The result – the supremely comfortable and welcoming living room in her New York State farmhouse – is ample testimony to her skills.

After much searching, Mary knew as soon as she saw it that this was the house she had always wanted. There had been a farmhouse on another part of the land but the building burned down in the 1890s, to be replaced by a long, low house connecting the two existing 1820s barns on the property. One barn – the location of the present living room – has been converted; the second awaits Mary's transforming talents.

When Mary bought the house, the living room with its low ceiling

looked dark and even lower than it actually was, thanks to the knotty pine panelling which covered all the walls. Mary's first challenge was to restore a feeling of light and correct the proportions of the room. The main structural changes fulfilled both purposes – adding French doors leading onto the

When it came to choosing the colours of the walls and woodwork, Mary decided to adopt a combination she had seen in a magazine picture of an Italian farmhouse – faded blue wood and yellow walls. As soon as the walls were painted, however, she realized her mistake. The yellow looked sickly. The alternative she chose picked up a soft pinky rose shade from the sofa upholstery. But, although she now knew that this was the right colour for the room, it proved to be rather elusive. There was no existing trade colour and even computer matching failed. Luckily, by happy accident, Mary discovered that applying a deep rose red over a cream background, and rubbing it in while the background was still wet, gave her just the colour and effect she wanted.

The other surfaces and finishes keep the emphasis firmly on comfort. The original brick floor is covered with a big textured ivory rug in front of the fire; a large squashy stool is upholstered with a kelim for informal lounging; there are deep armchairs and a sofa for relaxing. There are lamps for reading, uplighters in the corners for soft background illumination and tiny halogen bulbs – on dimmers – tucked into the angles of the beams for a magic, sparkling light at night.

terrace and installing more windows. However, these changes were expensive and forced economies in other areas.

All the pine panelling was taken down and the walls replastered. Floor-to-ceiling bookcases to house Mary's substantial library were fitted in round the windows, making them appear recessed and, by emphasizing the vertical, helping to counteract the natural lowness of the room. As to decoration, Mary knew that she wanted it to be as light and comfortable as possible. She rubbed white stain into the ceiling beams to fade them.

171

CHAPTER NINE

EVENING ENTERTAINING

YOU DON'T HAVE TO BE A SOCIAL BUTTERFLY TO HAVE A REASON FOR ENTERTAINING. EVEN IF YOU DO NOT GIVE MANY DINNER PARTIES, THERE IS THE YEARLY ROUND OF BIRTHDAYS, THE SEASONAL CELEBRATIONS OF CHRISTMAS, EASTER AND OTHER FESTIVALS, AND PERHAPS, ONCE IN A WHILE, A WEDDING. GOOD PLANNING AND ORGANIZATION WILL HELP YOU TO RISE TO THE OCCASION. BUT FOR THE PARTY TO BE A RESOUNDING SUCCESS IT IS EVEN MORE IMPORTANT TO EXERCISE IMAGINATION AND FLAIR.

Swags of greenery and bright red apples bobbing from a chandelier bring festive cheer to a hallway. Simple, striking ideas and natural ingredients are the essence of country entertaining.

CUT FLOWER STEMS
DIAGONALLY TO
PRESENT THE GREATEST
SURFACE AREA TO THE
WATER. STRIP LEAVES
FROM THE LOWER STEM
AND PLACE THE DISPLAY
AWAY FROM CHILLY
DRAUGHTS OR EXCESS
HEAT. TOP UP OR CHANGE
THE WATER EVERY DAY,
RETRIMMING STEMS FROM
TIME TO TIME.

SOCIAL EVENTS TURN THE HOUSE TOPSY-TURVY chiefly because few of us have the space to entertain properly. In the past, many houses included a room reserved for visitors, either a 'parlour' or a reception room which was outside the daily activities of the household. Nowadays, of course, this is rarely the case: the celebration has to be accommodated in the rooms you use every day. And if the occasion makes particular demands in terms of atmosphere or function, those rooms will have to be transformed on the spot. Much can be done with flowers, and the presentation of food is important. You can create instant effects with fabric or trimming. The crucial thing, however, is to have some unifying idea to tie it all together.

GETTING IDEAS

Some of the most successful parties involve no more in the way of forethought than setting out some nibbles and making sure there is enough wine to go around. But the really special occasions, the ones that linger in the memory, almost always have something extra, a touch of magic which makes the party sparkle and fizz.

The whole notion of party themes is fraught with danger: it is all too easy to go over the top or be heavy-handed and strike quite the wrong note. While a blatantly obvious theme can sometimes be fun in a kitsch kind of way, in most cases the theme should be understated and underplayed. The purpose is to give the event a sense of presence and a hint of theatricality. Seasonal celebrations such as Christmas and Easter come with all manner of associations and ideas, from traditional colours to familiar scents, flowers and food. In such cases, you may have to work quite hard to restore a sense of originality to the occasion.

Colour is a good place to start. A colour idea is a subtle way of giving any party a theme. Flower arrangements and table settings can be co-ordinated; even, to some, extent, food. Warm reds and greens are

The view from outside is an important part of creating a sense of welcome and hospitality (far left). Here candles light a display of gourds and squash, an effective suggestion of harvest plenty.

Christmas is the time to go over the top – literally – with boughs of greenery, trailing ivy wound round the window frames and bright accents of red berries and apples, all softened in the glow of candlelight (left).

175

WINTER IS A LEAN TIME IN THE GARDEN AND THE FEW FLOWERS AVAILABLE INCLUDE SNOWDROPS, WINTER JASMINE, HELLEBORE, WINTER SWEET AND IRIS. SUPPLEMENT THEM WITH BERRIES SUCH AS COTONEASTER AND SKIMMIA, AND WITH INTERESTING FOLIAGE.

natural choices for Christmas and winter parties, set off with silver or gold for a glittering occasion. Easter colours are blue, mauve and yellow, the colours of spring. Russets, browns and bronzes are autumnal in spirit; in summer the riot of colour in the garden gives plenty of choice.

Colour does not have to be seasonal, however. You might choose the colours of a team or a school; or a child's favourite colour for a birthday theme. Colour can also be used to emphasize the existing colours of the interior, either as a sharp, invigorating accent – a splash of red tulips in a pale-toned room – or blending with it.

In the country, a party theme might arise simply out of nature and the particular time of year. Decorate the house with branches, foliage, fruit and berries, as well as flowers, to bring a sense of the outdoors into the heart of the occasion. Spring blossom, pumpkins and gourds, vines and ivy, winter branches bring their own seasonal associations.

Some associations – and accessories – are unavoidable. The tree at Christmas, Easter eggs in baskets, hearts on Valentine's Day, Hallowe'en jack-o'-lanterns, the Guy Fawkes bonfire are all indelibly written into each event and could never be happily omitted. But to inject a little element of surprise you might tinker with presentation just to keep the decorations from being too safe and expected. Instead of one big Christmas tree, for example, you might have a few small ones glowing in alcoves; similarly, a line of grinning pumpkins in the window has infinitely more impact than one. Coloured eggs can be hidden all around the room in odd places at Easter time; the heart

Seasonal flower arrangements keep pace with the year and draw the world outside closer. A delicate winter arrangement of white Christmas roses, snowdrops and silvery foliage is displayed in vials next to a vase of white hyacinths (above left). The warm autumnal tints of dried flowers and foliage frame a painted panel and harmonize with the ochre sideboard (below left). In the summer white flowers set off with dark green foliage look fresh and cool (below). White flowers also show up well on the long summer evenings, as the light fades. Spring arrangements, like this basket of amaryllis, can be living displays of planted bulbs (below right). Hyacinths, muscari, snowdrops and crocus are all equally effective.

theme on Valentine's Day can be extended to the presentation of food and drink. On Bonfire Night, you might run a string of fairy lights round the room as a reminder of the fireworks outside.

FLOWERS AND ALL THE TRIMMINGS

Flowers have a big role to play when you are decorating the house for any social event. They are relatively cheap, especially if you can supplement florist's flowers with material from your own garden, and they are quick to assemble, transforming a room in a matter of minutes. When the party is over you can hand out individual blooms as a favour to departing guests. Flowers are also one of the most evocative ways of tying an event into the time of year.

To dry HYDRANGEA HEADS, LEAVE THE FLOWERS IN A VASE WITH ABOUT 5 CM (2 IN) WATER. THEY WILL DRY GRADUALLY AS THE WATER IS DRUNK. TO KEEP PETALS SOFT AND FLEXIBLE, ADD A SMALL AMOUNT OF GLYCERINE TO THE WATER, IN THE RATIO OF ONE TO THREE.

Party flowers differ from arrangements which you would create for everyday enjoyment. First of all, they have to be noticed in a room full of people, which usually means that displays must be larger and fuller, perhaps also more emphatic in colour. Secondly, they need to be out of the way so that containers are not toppled over by people backing into unsteady tables. The mantelpiece – on the eye level of standing guests – is often ideal; in the summer, a hearth could also be filled with flowers. Alcoves and spaces on book shelves are other good positions. You can also hang flowers from an archway, twine a garland up a banister or loop foliage across an entrance.

To keep displays affordable, it is better to concentrate on acquiring a quantity of cheap flowers rather than spending a fortune on a negligible amount of exotic blooms. Select the same variety or colour for maximum impact and supplement arrangements with foliage – ivy, evergreen cuttings, branches from shrubs and bushes, for example. Wide ribbon, twists of fabric and other types of dress trimming are also useful for making flowers go further. Add plaid bows for Christmas, red velvet for Valentine's Day, or silvery satin for a christening.

Wedding flowers have to be right. Aside from the sheer emotional impact of the day, wedding displays invariably form the backdrop to many of the wedding photographs and will accordingly be preserved forever on film. Flowers for a reception at home or in a marquee set up in the garden can harmonize with the colour of the bride's dress or the dresses of her bridesmaids, or echo in content or colour the bridal bouquet.

Whatever the occasion, flowers are a natural accompaniment to food; in fact, flowers and food can often be combined to great effect in a table centre. For a seated dinner party, keep the flowers low and trailing rather than high or wide, so that they do not obstruct conversation. And avoid overly scented flowers which might clash unpleasantly with the aroma of food or drink. Individual floral place settings are an attractive idea, especially if each vase or container varies slightly from its neighbour. Don't forget to add flowers to a buffet table or serving table; obviously these arrangements can be larger and taller since there are no views to impede. And you can extend the

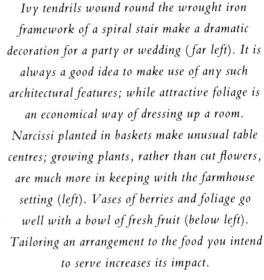

Ivy tendrils wound round the wrought iron framework of a spiral stair make a dramatic decoration for a party or wedding (far left). It is always a good idea to make use of any such architectural features; while attractive foliage is an economical way of dressing up a room. Narcissi planted in baskets make unusual table centres; growing plants, rather than cut flowers, are much more in keeping with the farmhouse setting (left). Vases of berries and foliage go well with a bowl of fresh fruit (below left). Tailoring an arrangement to the food you intend to serve increases its impact.

floral theme by adding individual flower heads, or petals, or leaves to serving dishes, platters or drinks trays. For more of a period look, swagged foliage or garlands can be hung around the perimeter of a serving table, bound around columns or trailed around doorways for added emphasis.

It may sound like gilding the lily, but flower arrangements are also indispensable for an outdoor party. Again, it is a question of emphasis. If your garden is flourishing and your borders are well stocked, you might simply put together a few displays which represent in miniature the glories all around. Fill baskets or terracotta pots with your selection and place them around the terrace or on the table where food is set out. Alternatively, you might pick out a single colour and base your displays on that. Containers can be as rough and ready as you like: flower pots, baskets, metal watering cans and wooden tubs are all at home outdoors.

To make crystallized flower heads and petals, prepare a mixture of 50 g (2 oz) gum arabic and 4 tsp rosewater and leave to stand overnight. Dip the flowers in the mixture, then in caster sugar, and allow to dry. Primroses, violets, roses, nasturtiums and sweet peas can be treated in this way and used to decorate gifts or place settings. Nasturtiums are edible so can also be used to decorate food.

It is also important to remember that you should try to make guests feel welcome from the moment they arrive. Flowers at the entrance, either in the hall, flanking the door or in the form of a wreath or garland tied to the front door introduce the party and give some idea of what's to come. Ideally, such displays should echo the decorations in the rest of the house. Door wreaths always seem to suggest Christmas and evergreens, but they can be made of almost any foliage, flowers, herbs or even fruits for a variety of seasonal flavours. And door decorations don't have to be in the form of a circle, either: a posy tied to a door knocker is equally charming.

SETTING THE SCENE

The focal point of most parties, at some point, will be the table where food is served or enjoyed. The presentation of food is another area where the minimum of effort can make a great difference to the way the occasion is experienced.

Tables generally need to be covered with some kind of cloth. If the table has a fine polished surface a cloth over a padded layer underneath will protect it from heat and moisture; if the table is less precious, a cloth will transform it into something which looks more elegant. And if you need to push two tables together to seat everyone, a cloth can help to disguise the join. The traditional formal tablecloth is white damask, handed down from generation to generation and lovingly laundered until it is as soft as silk. Lace is another heirloom cloth, laid over plain white or ivory linen. With the emphasis on elegance and refinement, lay the table with a matching dinner service and fine crystal glasses.

Less formally, the cloth can be coloured or printed. A simple length of cotton dyed the appropriate shade will fit in with a party that has a dominant colour theme. You can also buy cheap bolts of cloth from market stalls to give a table an instant facelift. Matching cloth napkins can be run up very easily on the sewing machine. For informal gatherings, try ikat patterns, gingham, stripes, or any traditional folk patterns such as the Soleiado prints from Provence. For a buffet or large dinner party, serve food imaginatively, taking the trouble to match the colour of the food to dishes or add sprigs of fresh herbs or flower petals as decoration. There is no need to carve radishes into intricate shapes or to sculpt the butter – natural and fresh-looking garnishes can make a serving dish much more appealing. Avoid the tired sprig of parsley or the lone lemon slice; try sprinklings of chopped fresh chives, basil leaves, generous chunks of lemon or lime, edible flowers like nasturtiums, and purple-veined cabbage leaves to edge a plate instead of lettuce. If, as the saying goes, you eat with your eyes, treat your guests to a feast of colour and pattern!

A beautiful crewel work tablecloth is almost all the decoration needed in this panelled dining-room. Blue side plates and the mellow rust red of celosia in individual vases pick up the colours of the embroidery; dried hydrangeas in similarly muted shades look stately flanking the mantelpiece.

Lee Bailey's Long Island Hospitality

Every weekend the writer and designer Lee Bailey leaves the city for his house on the shore of Long Island, overlooking the Atlantic Ocean. Along this stretch of coastline, as at Martha's Vineyard and Nantucket, there are glacial ponds, small freshwater lakes which extend right up to the water's edge, separated from the sea only by a strip of dune. Lee is fortunate enough to live in a house located where Sagg Pond, one of these unusual natural features, joins the ocean. Like the foothills of an immense mountain range, the pond's smaller scale softens the enormity of the ocean.

The house, modern, plain and functional, has been designed, decorated and furnished to keep the attention firmly focused on the spectacular views. In the living room, furniture is grouped round the large wood-burning fireplace with its angular black steel hood and brick hearth. The generous, comfortable stools and sofas are upholstered in painter's linen, a robust material in natural white; the floor is covered with a flat, hard-wearing carpet in 'banker's grey' with woven cotton washable rugs defining the seating areas; the coffee table is an old captain's chest.

This neutral background, fresh and simple like much of Lee's work, is the perfect foil for the dramatic ocean views. Sliding doors lead to decks which run down to the water's edge, giving a great sense of connection with the outdoors. In the dining-room – virtually a glass box – glass is again used to dissolve the distinction between inside and outside space. At night, the room is lit from both indoors and out so that the glass remains transparent and does not

Lee's style of entertaining is relaxed and uncomplicated. He generally dispenses with any kind of first course, concentrating his efforts on a main dish, with intriguing accompaniments; and salad, in the European manner, comes after dinner. He tries to plan meals so that food can be prepared or almost finished in advance, so that he need not spend too much time in the kitchen when guests arrive. Friends may occasionally be called upon to shell peas, but otherwise Lee is a singleminded, well-organized cook who relishes creating an impression of effortlessness – one of the best ways, after all, of making your guests feel really welcome.

To end the meal, there is often some kind of wonderful, utterly indulgent dessert. Then, after dinner, there will be coffee and drinks in front of the fire. For large gatherings, Lee may serve a Southern-style shortcut – coffee, brandy and dessert all in one. His spiced coffee is a lethal New Orleans mixture of iced coffee, brandy, orange rind, cinnamon, cloves and sugar, served in champagne flutes or pilsner glasses.

This easy, informal attitude – to decoration as much as to entertaining – perfectly complements the elemental setting of the house, with its open views of sea and sky.

read like a blank black wall.

During the summer months especially, the house becomes a setting for entertaining. Weekend guests arrive in anticipation of Lee's cooking, which leans heavily on traditional recipes from his native New Orleans and is often based on seasonal produce, particularly the wonderful fresh vegetables sold from countless local roadside stands.

LIGHTING UP

Atmospheric lighting is essential for capturing the right mood, whether you are hosting a formal dinner party or an impromptu gathering for friends. You won't want to change the wall colour for the sake of a single evening, or take down the curtains, but quite subtle alterations to the lighting arrangement can make a room seem dramatically different.

Firelight and candlelight are the easiest and most effective means of injecting a look of mystery and atmosphere into the most mundane of settings. In a living room, leave a few lamps burning low and supplement them with a mass of candles arranged on a mantelpiece, side table or from one side of the hearth to the other if the fireplace is not

184

Lighting, particularly candlelight and firelight, is an important way of changing mood and atmosphere. Antique fittings make warm pools of light in a beamed hall, enriching the tones of the woollen tablecloth (far left). A floor-level arrangement focuses the attention on an elegant fireplace (centre). With sidelights on the mantelpiece and a large gilded mirror to add glitter and sparkle, the effect is one of great warmth and richness. Fading light on a summer evening is supplemented by the gentle glow of candlelight, on the table and above in the candelabra, as well as table lamps on side tables (above). A decorative wire sconce supports a candle for atmospheric lighting (left).

185

being used. Choose candles and candlesticks of the same material, colour and height for a stately look of period elegance; vary the type and size and arrange them in informal groups for a more homely effect. Candles also look extremely romantic when arranged in rows along a table top or the top of a chest, the flickering flames creating a dancing line of soft light.

Candles are an unbeatable way of creating a feeling of intimacy at the dinner table. In the country, keep candlesticks and candelabra unfussy and classic in design. Plain

Firelight and candles in staggered heights along the mantelpiece transform an old beamed room into an evocative, even mysterious setting for a dinner party (below). One small table lamp has been positioned behind a large arrangement of branches and foliage where it will throw interesting patterns of shadows on the wall. A roof garden is the romantic setting for a twilight supper (right). Candles, set in glasses to protect them from the wind, decorate the table with little points of light.

MANY TRADITIONAL CANDLE SCONCES HAVE MIRRORED BACKS. ON THE SAME PRINCIPLE, ARRANGE GROUPS OF CANDLES OF DIFFERENT HEIGHTS IN FRONT OF A MIRROR, OR ON A WINDOWSILL, TO DOUBLE THE LIGHT AND SPARKLE.

metal branched candelabra are widely available; there are also glass, brass and turned wooden holders. Excellent versions of the simple metal Shaker-style chandelier are also on the market: soft candlelight twinkling overhead is perhaps the most magical atmospheric light of all.

Evening parties outdoors offer more opportunities for theatrical effects with light. Even if you haven't installed a permanent form of garden lighting, you can still arrange attractive temporary illumination of the main seating and eating areas with a minimum of difficulty.

You might like to run festive strings of fairy lights along a garden wall, in the trees or around a barbecue area (make sure you use a waterproof connection for safety). Candles also look great outdoors, especially when darkness has fallen. On a warm still night, ordinary household candles can be massed on a table or around the perimeter of a terrace; if the conditions are windier, nightlights shining in little glass dishes can be placed in atmospheric groups or down the side of a flight of steps to pick out a pathway. And Chinese paper lanterns, glowing with light and hanging from a line threaded through the trees, turn any garden into a very special outdoor room.

Henrietta Green's Table of Delights

Henrietta Green is a food writer and broadcaster whose special area of interest, fresh ingredients and speciality produce, has taken her to farms, local shops and producers all over Britain, as well as further afield. A real enthusiast and connoisseur of good food, her forays in search of information for her books and programmes have provided a wonderful opportunity to sample the most delicious and interesting food in the country.

Such delights as fresh Norfolk ice cream, home-cured Shropshire bacon, dried Portuguese figs and farmhouse cheeses are likely to end up gracing the dining table in her London flat, to the enviable enjoyment of her guests. Although Henrietta is London-based, she has created a real sense of country living in the heart of the city, an atmosphere which owes as much to her attitude of easy hospitality as to the light decoration of the dining-room and her collection of old blue and white china.

The focus of interest in her dining-room is the circular oak table with its central feature, a low terracotta pot of ivy which stays on the table year round, fronds and tendrils reaching out in all directions. A living centrepiece such as this costs less than fresh flowers and makes the table look

furnished even when it is not in use. A naturally low-growing and trailing variety should be chosen to keep views free across the table. Berries, fruit or little glass vases of flowers can be added to dress up the table for a special occasion.

Encircling the ivy is a collection of unusual pieces of china and glass dishes filled with all kinds of treats for guests to nibble. Henrietta often uses two candle-lit lanterns

and several more candlesticks to set the scene, with a dimmable chandelier overhead to keep the light low and intimate.

Henrietta is a firm believer in keeping the table filled with appetizing goodies that delight the eye as much as the palate. As she hates to see bare space, each inch of the table is covered with dishes, often several courses at the same time so that guests feel free to help themselves whenever they want. A pretty table filled to overflowing instantly makes guests feel welcome; even informal suppers provide occasions for Henrietta to indulge her friends with unusual or simply delicious discoveries brought back from her trips or made in her own kitchen.

What she serves depends on the time of year and where she has recently visited: there might be crystallized greengages, raisins on stalks, macaroons, sweetmeats, little soft cheeses and home-made water biscuits. A memorable find from Italy were little individual sugar cases which melted in the mouth to release pure flavours of rose petal, violet or coffee. And on most occasions, there will be different kinds of bread, as well as salad which she buys from a good local market served in a favourite slipware bowl.

The table is set with white Davenport, supplemented with a

collection of blue and white china in subtly mismatched patterns. Pasta and stews are served up in large Victorian soup bowls, each with a different pattern. And there are also blue and white tureens, some of which may sit empty on the table just for display.

The decor of the room, light and understated, keeps the attention focused on the table. Ivory walls match cream chintz curtains which

hang to the ground; the cornice, dado rail and woodwork are picked out in white. The huge casement window was lowered to the ground to provide better views of the neighbouring gardens. Numerous pots on the small balcony add to the greenery.

The French marble fireplace is flanked by two dried standard box and eucalyptus trees. In the winter a welcoming gas log fire glows in

the hearth; in the summer, the fireplace is covered with an antique needlework firescreen.

Winter or summer, the ivy remains on the dining table. At Christmas time, Henrietta tucks sprigs of holly among the fronds and hides sweets for children to find. More practical than fresh flowers and more unusual than dried, the ivy keeps the table looking welcoming all year round.

189

INDEX

ACKNOWLEDGMENTS

The publisher thanks the following photographers and organizations for their permission to reproduce the photographs in this book:

1 René Stoeltie; 2 Photography Rodney Weidland, Courtesy Belle Magazine; 3 Yves Duronsoy; 4–5 IPC Magazines/WPN; 6–7 Photography Rodney Weidland, Courtesy Belle Magazine; 8 Jean-Pierre Godeaut; 10 René Stoeltie; 11 Christian Sarramon; 12 Yves Duronsoy; 12–13 Paul Ryan/J.B. Visual Press; 14 Fritz von der Schulenburg (Jill de Brand); 15 Peter Woloszynski/EWA (Elizabeth Whiting & Associates); 16–17 Christian Sarramon; 17 above Ianthe Ruthven; 17 below Paul Ryan/J.B. Visual Press; 18 left Dennis Krukowski; 18 right Christian Sarramon; 19 Marie-Louise Avery; 20 IPC Magazines/WPN; 21 Yves Duronsoy; 22–3 Paul Ryan/J.B. Visual Press; 24 Derry Moore; 25 Stylograph/Beaufre; 26 David Phelps; 27 Yves Duronsoy; 28 Gilles de Chabaneix; 29 above Fritz von der Schulenburg (Karl-Heinz Scherer); 29 below Michael Freeman; 30 Ken Kirkwood; 30–31 Paul Ryan/J.B. Visual Press; 32 Peter Rauter; 33 Yves Duronsoy; 34 Guy Bouchet; 35 Christian Sarramon; 37 World of Interiors/John Vere Brown; 38–39 Jean-Pierre Godeaut; 39 René Stoeltie; 40 below Michael Freeman; 40 above left and above right IPC Magazines/WPN; 41 above and below Yves Duronsoy; 42–3 Richard Bryant/Arcaid; 43 Jean-Paul Bonhommet; 44–5 Paul Ryan/J.B. Visual Press; 45 Jean-Paul Bonhommet; 46–7 Ken Kirkwood; 48 Jean-Paul Bonhommet; 49 Tom Leighton/EWA; 50 above Yves Duronsoy; 50 IPC Magazines/WPN; 51 Fritz von der Schulenburg; 52 above Jean-Paul Bonhommet; 52 below Guy Bouchet; 53 Stafford Cliff; 54–55 Chris Mead; 57 Di Lewis/Elizabeth Whiting & Associates; 58–59 Rodney Hyett/EWA; 59 above Christian Sarramon; 59 below Gilles de Chabaneix; 60 above & below Paul Ryan/J.B. Visual Press; 61 Camera Press; 62 Jean-Paul Bonhommet; 63 Fritz von der Schulenburg (The indoor room. Nessa O'Neill); 64 Bent Rej; 65 Marie-Louise Avery; 66 left René Stoeltie; 66 right Christian Sarramon; 67 Jean-Paul Bonhommet; 70–1 Ianthe Ruthven; 71 Yves Duronsoy; 72 Peter Woloszynski/EWA; 73 Lars Hallen; 74 Fritz von der Schulenburg (Emma Bini); 75 Jean-Paul Bonhommet; 76–7 Jerry Harpur; 78 IPC Magazines/WPN; 79 Marie-Louise Avery; 80 Andreas von Einsiedel/EWA; 81 Fritz von der Schulenburg (Jill de Brand); 82–3 Yves Duronsoy; 84–5 Paul Ryan/J.B. Visual Press; 85 Jean-Paul Bonhommet; 86 left Amparo Garrida; 86 right Tom Leighton/EWA; 87 Arcaid/Niall Clutton; 88 Ianthe Ruthven; 89 Arcaid/Richard Bryant; 90 Camera Press; 91 IPC Magazines/WPN; 92 left Tim Street Porter/EWA; 92 right Steve Colby/EWA; 93 Ianthe Ruthven; 94 Yves Duronsoy; 95 Fritz von der Schulenburg (Suky Schellenberg); 96–7 Tom Eckerle; 98 IPC Magazines/WPN; 99 Yves Duronsoy; 100–1 Tim Street Porter/EWA; 102 above Fritz von der Schulenburg (John Stefanidis); 102 below Christian Sarramon; 103 Jean-Paul Bonhommet; 104 above Mike Nich-olson/EWA; 104 below IPC Magazines/WPN; 105 Yves Duronsoy; 106–7 Stylograph/Godeaut; 108 Andreas von Einsiedel/EWA; 109 René Stoeltie; 110 above Jean-Paul Bonhommet; 110 below Tim Street Porter/EWA; 111 Dia Press/Torsten Hogh; 112–113 John Hollingshead/Conran Octopus; 114 Christian Sarramon; 115 Yves Duronsoy; 116–7 Spike Powell/EWA; 117 Christian Sarramon; 118–9 World of Interiors/James Mortimer; 119 right Andreas von Einsiedel/EWA; 120 above Christian Sarramon; 120 below Jean-Paul Bonhommet; 121 Peter Aprahamian/EWA; 122 René Stoeltie; 123 above Bent Rej; 123 below Nadia Mackenzie; 124 Peter Woloszynski/EWA; 125 René Stoeltie; 126 Yves Duronsoy; 127 above left Christian Sarramon; 127 above right Jean-Paul Bonhommet; 127 below Christian Sarramon; 128 La Maison de Marie Claire/Hoeppe/Saulnier/Bayle; 130 Victor Watts/EWA; 131 above Tom Leighton/EWA; 131 below Yves Duronsoy; 132–133 Tom Eckerle; 134 Stylograph/Brackrock; 135 Ianthe Ruthven; 136/7 Spike Powell/EWA; 138 IPC Magazines/WPN; 139 World of Interiors/James Mortimer; 140 Christian Sarramon; 141 above Vogue Living/Raffaele Origonee; 141 below Fritz von der Schulenburg (Piers von Westenholz); 142 above Guy Bouchet; 142 below Yves Duronsoy; 142–3 Nadia Mackenzie; 144 Jan Baldwin; 145 left René Stoeltie; 145 right Jan Baldwin; 146 Fritz von der Schulenburg (Juliette Mole); 147 IPC Magazines/WPN; 147 below left Guy Bouchet; 147 below right Jean-Pierre Godeaut; 148 above Pia Tryde; 148 below Yves Duronsoy; 149 World of Interiors/Tim Beddow; 150 above Christian Sarramon; 150 IPC Magazines/WPN; 151 Paul Ryan/J.B. Visual Press; 152 Paul Ryan/JB Visual Press; 153 Fritz von der Schulenburg; 154–5 IPC Magazines/WPN; 156 Jean-Paul Bonhommet; 157 Ken Kirkwood; 158 Ianthe Ruthven; 159 Fritz von der Schulenburg (Laura Ashley); 160 Paul Ryan/JB Visual Press; 161 René Stoeltie; 162 Paul Barker; 163 above Karen Bussolini; 163 below Nadia Mackenzie; 164–5 Pia Tryde; 166 Jean-Paul Bonhommet; 167 left Yves Duronsoy; 167 right Christian Sarramon; 168–9 Paul Ryan; 170 Bill Stites/Conran Octopus; 170–1 Kurt Dolnier; 172 IPC Magazines/WPN; 173 Yves Duronsoy; 174 left Dia Press; 174–175 IPC Magazines/WPN; 176 above Linda Burgess/Conran Octopus; 176 below La Maison de Marie Claire/Beaufre/Peuch; 177 left Pia Tryde; 177 right Fritz von der Schulenburg (Ken Turner); 178 IPC Magazines/WPN; 179 above IPC Magazines/WPN; 179 below Fritz von der Schulenburg (Juliette Mole); 181 Fritz von der Schulenburg (Andrea de Montal); 182–3 Tom Eckerle; 184 left Yves Duronsoy; 184–5 Yves Duronsoy; 185 above Bent Rej; 185 below Spike Powell/EWA; 186 IPC Magazines/WPN; 187 Peter Rauter; 188–9 Paul Ryan/J.B. Visual Press.

Every effort has been made to trace the copyright holders and we apologise in advance for any unintentional omission. We would be pleased to insert the appropriate acknowledgment in any subsequent edition of this publication.